Medical Spanish Mix and Match

Easy Spanish for Health Care Professionals

©Murnez Blades

Combine sentence structures to communicate clearly, confidently, and accurately in Spanish. This book includes clinical history and intake exams with yes/no and short answers and procedural explanations with sample translations. Use with the *Spanish for Fun and Forever* CD.

iUniverse LLC
Bloomington

MEDICAL SPANISH MIX AND MATCH
EASY SPANISH FOR HEALTH CARE PROFESSIONALS

iUniverse books may be ordered through booksellers or by contacting:

iUniverse
1663 Liberty Drive
Bloomington, IN 47403
www.iuniverse.com
1-800-Authors (1-800-288-4677)

ISBN: 978-1-4917-1736-3 (sc)
ISBN: 978-1-4917-1737-0 (hc)
ISBN: 978-1-4917-1738-7 (e)

Library of Congress Control Number: 2013922204

Printed in the United States of America.

iUniverse rev. date: 2/26/2014

Dedicated to Carol Beck

For her selfless love, dedication,
encouragement, patience, and kindness.

For the example of a strong
yet gentle leader and lady.

Acknowledgments

I had the good fortune to work with editor Lizette Shinmachi. She prepared this book for publication by reorganizing, formatting tables and graphics, and editing content for *Medical Spanish Mix and Match*.

My sincere thanks also go to Dr. Michelle Molina for her encouragement and support. I express my gratitude to Shari Dadfar for her inspiration.

Contents

Chapter 1: Why You Should Use This Book

Welcome

This book provides you with effective tools to communicate in Spanish with your patients. Read this chapter to help yourself use these tools more successfully. This information on communication, respect in Hispanic culture, and the nature of learning will make it easier for you to learn Spanish and speak it with your patients.

Learn to greet and part appropriately; to extract the information you need from your patients; and to further develop your Spanish skills.

Your Goal Is Successful Communication

Have you ever heard or said, "I studied Spanish for years and couldn't speak a word"? Or have you decided that it is too difficult to learn Spanish because you are too old and children learn better and faster?

The solution is simple: *Communication, not perfection, is your goal!* Make communication your goal and learn Spanish in the same manner as children learn it. Your result? Successful communication in Spanish.

Communication and Language

The majority (90 percent) of your communication is nonverbal.[1] Of this, 30 percent is your intonation, and the remainder is body language. Your words represent only 10 percent (some say 7 percent) of your communication!

Success with Nonverbal Communication

Do you realize that babies are always communicating with you through body language? Children hear and understand before they can speak. The baby may slap at the bottle or push it away. If uncomfortable, the *bebé* cries.

Success with Verbal Communication

Young mothers today use sign language to communicate with babies as young as six months of age. At a party I attended one weekend, a young mother, having just fed her baby, intuited and confirmed via sign language that the baby just wanted the *chupete* (pacifier) and not more food. Sign language, an aspect of body language, created successful communication. As a result, both Mommy and baby were happy.

Your patients will be equally happy and appreciative if you communicate with them in Spanish, however simply. Like communication with babies, you will begin with simple expressions—one word or phrase. Your efforts will be immediately rewarded with a smile or a gesture. *Wow! This person cares about me enough to try to communicate,* the patient says to himself or herself.

Why You Want to Use Spanish

Despite the fact that many native speakers bring an interpreter or that you may have one, your efforts to communicate are a powerful, heartfelt message: *I care about you!* The respect that you will give your patients through your efforts will be invaluable.

Immediate Success with This Book

This book's goal is to teach you to communicate with *a few clear words*. To succeed, you *keep your communication simple*.

Why? If you use too many words, you may miscommunicate. Or your listener may believe you understand everything and overwhelm you with a barrage of words.

In this book you will use simple, direct methods to learn medical Spanish. No complex grammar rules. No memorization of verb conjugations. You can use this book to be courteous and begin communicating immediately.

Learning Methods Determine Learning Success

How We Adults Learn

We adults focus on perfection. We write the answers. We worry what others will think. We are inhibited about responding. We memorize vocabulary in a straightforward, boring way. We worry about what we do not know instead of paying attention to what we are learning.

How Children Learn

Children learn language faster than adults do. Why? Children employ a variety of learning activities. These activities include right-brained, creative functions that imprint on the left brain.

- Children sing songs, which opens both brain hemispheres. The rhythm imprints the words, pronunciations, and sentence patterns into the children's memories.
- Children play learning games, which provide repetition and fun. Repetition puts facts into our memory and builds useful habits.[2] Fun relaxes us so that we learn new information and skills more easily and quickly.[3]

- Children use vision, touch, and action to learn vocabulary. They identify pictures, touch body parts, and act out verbs. In this way they directly connect words with the physical reality.

Children are absorbed in the activity that produces language learning. All their energy goes into that activity.

Results of Learning Methods

The following diagram[4] illustrates how different methods of learning determine how much language we remember after twenty-four hours.

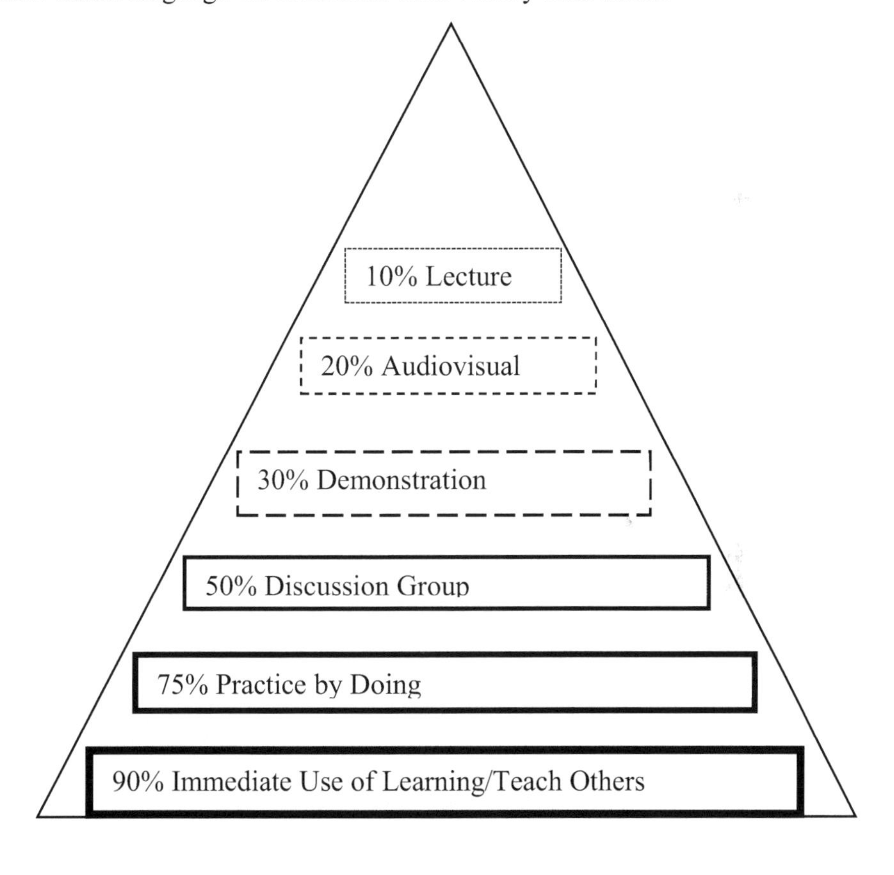

After twenty-four hours, we remember 90 percent of all words that we see, say, and hear ***while speaking Spanish.*** That is why we learn best by speaking aloud while we read and touch the words and while we stand up, walk, and/or tap while saying the words. This is the reason that you will learn Spanish more easily and quickly if you always follow the practice directions in this book.

Learning Methods in This Book

You are going to learn the way our children learn—through fun, music, and action.

Why Fun?

Our attention and energy are naturally drawn to fun activities, and learning requires our attention and energy. Fun is an instant reward that motivates us to repeat the activity, and repetition assists learning. Fun relaxes us and dissolves fear and self-criticism. Our comfortable engagement makes our minds open and flexible. We naturally learn more and learn it more easily.[5]

Why Music?

In chapter 14 of Eric Jensen's *Brain-Based Learning*, we learn that both sides of the brain are involved in processing music. The pulse of the body (heart rate) tends to synchronize with the beat of the music; the faster the music, the faster the pulse. Music relaxes the learners and stimulates the limbic region of the brain that affects long-term memory. This combination of language with music dramatically increases motivation and learning. Many of us have heard of the "Mozart" effect.[6]

Because music is so useful in enhancing our learning process, the CD *Spanish for Fun and Forever* was created to add fun and interest to your learning experience. The lyrics to the tracks on this CD are presented in chapter 5.

Why Action?

Using physical actions to learn Spanish is based on the strategy of Total Physical Response (known as TPR).[7] This is a right-brained approach to second-language learning. It was researched and popularized by Dr. James J. Asher, professor of psychology. "TPR (total physical response) is a method of teaching language using physical movement to react to verbal input in order to reduce student inhibitions and lower their affective filter. It allows students to react to language without thinking too much, facilitates long term retention, and reduces student anxiety and stress. In order to implement TPR effectively, it is necessary to plan regular sessions that progress in a logical order, and to keep several principles in mind."[8]

Methods Used in This Book

With the TPR method, you first respond physically to commands, which most students enjoy doing. Then you develop a large vocabulary and become comfortable speaking through practice. Thus, in this book, you will use the following:

- Music and TPR to learn basic vocabulary
- Visual/touch method to learn additional vocabulary

Next, you will learn to communicate with the mix-and-match method as follows:

- Learn a few basic patterns and begin to manipulate them.
- Work in pairs to practice some basic conversations.
- Practice structuring your own communication.

Respect for Native Healing—Curanderismo

What Is "Curanderismo" and Why Do I Need to Know about It?

A *curandero* or *curandera* (native healer) is the cultural and spiritual community leader who knows the curative powers of many plants. Spanish-speaking clients visit him or her for help with physical, emotional, and spiritual problems. Therefore, your patients may fear doctors and unfamiliar equipment and practices. A wise English-speaking caregiver speaks respectfully of the curandero, which helps gain the patient's confidence.

Often, patients are taking natural herbs given by the curandero. These medicines could be contraindications of prescribed medicines and may cause a lethal reaction. In order for the patient to feel confident enough to disclose all medicines taken, the physician must gain the trust of the patient by being respectful of his or her beliefs.

Native healing (*curanderismo*) is a diverse system that incorporates "el don" (the gift) from God with methods handed down by the ancestors. Methods from Native America, Spain, Mexico, and Africa are included. Most healers believe that they are living channels of divine energy and that they are able to increase the health and well-being of the client.

Healers believe that illness comes from an imbalance in the mind that affects the body. Intense emotions caused by trauma (e.g., divorce or an accident) or a specific event (e.g., fire, earthquake, or car accident) could cause such an imbalance. Anxiety accompanied by symptoms such as insomnia, diarrhea, extreme nervousness, sadness, depression, and loss of appetite would be treated with herbal medicine, massage, and prayer.

"In Western medicine the body goes to the hospital, the mind to the psychiatrist, and the soul and spirit to church. In curanderismo, the healing takes place under one roof," says Elena Avila, a psychiatric nurse specialist, curandera, and author of *Woman Who Glows in the Dark.*[9]

How to Use This Medical Spanish Book

Read each section and do its practice exercises, in the following sequence:

1. Learn Spanish pronunciation and greetings.
2. Learn Spanish vocabulary for the content you need to use.
3. Use the two-part and three-part tables to communicate in Spanish.

Use the Mix-and-Match System in This Book

Sentence beginning + action word + sentence ending (as needed)

To comment or question, use these tables to create a sentence that contains two parts (beginning + action word) or three parts (beginning + action word + ending). Use an ending when needed in your sentence or question. Following are three-part and two-part examples. (Note that, combined with the infinitive, *favor de* is the equivalent of the English *please*. This structure is an alternative to the direct command form and is not only more polite but also easier to use.)

Beginning	Action Word	Ending (as needed)
Favor de Please	**mover** to move	**la mano.** your hand.
Es necesario It is necessary	**relajar.** to relax.	

Mix-and-Match Benefits

- No verb conjugation
- No grammar

So how do you learn to communicate quickly, without memorizing many forms for each verb? You use simple, clear communication. For example, to communicate, “Please eat now,” you say, “Favor de *comer* ahora.”

This approach is built into the tables in this book. Then you can mix and match words from the table columns and communicate immediately, clearly, and simply. (Note: Many Asian languages use a similar system as in the mix-and-match tables. They do not alter verbs to indicate the subject or time of the action.)

Compare the simplicity of using the mix-and-match tables to communicate with the traditional emphasis on grammar as shown in the following table.

In Present-Tense Spanish		**In Past-Tense Spanish**	
Como I eat	**Comemos** We eat	**Comí** I ate	**Comimos** We ate
Comes You (one person) eat	**Comeis** You (two people) eat	**Comiste** You (one person) ate	**Comisteis** You (two people) ate
Come She/he eats	**Comen** They eat	**Comió** She/he ate	**Comieron** They ate

Chapter 2: Preparing to Speak Spanish

Why Learn Correct Pronunciation?

Saying Spanish word sounds correctly is an important part of communicating clearly. Your patients will appreciate understanding you immediately as you speak. They will be able to focus on what you are telling them instead of struggling to figure out what you are saying. Their understanding of your words will simplify your communication with them as you treat them.

Your Reward

You can review an intake exam in Spanish with a patient as soon as you master Spanish pronunciation using this chapter.

Important: Use These Exercises!

This part of learning Spanish requires lots of repetition because you are building new pronunciation habits. Your tongue and mouth need the practice to become comfortable making these new sounds. Your mind needs the practice to automatically think in Spanish sounds. Repeat this pronunciation practice daily until you automatically pronounce these Spanish words correctly.

Be Successful

If you have five minutes to review a letter section, practice speaking the words. The more you practice, the more relaxed and fluent your pronunciation will become.

Consider each practice session a little game. Decide to enjoy it, and you will. The fun you experience makes your new pronunciation habit easier to remember and to repeat.

Be pleased with yourself for each practice session you do. You are creating a stronger Spanish toolset for yourself each time. Approval of your own efforts builds your self-confidence in speaking Spanish words, and your increased self-confidence makes it easier for you to communicate clearly with your patients.

Pronounce Spanish Vowels

The vowels in Spanish are always pronounced the same way in every word in which they are used.

a (ah) as in *father*

e (eh) as in *met*

i (ee) as in *keep*

o (oh) as in *open*

u (oo) as in *tool*

Directions

1. Slowly say each vowel sound in the preceding list, and notice how you open your mouth and shape your lips to say the vowel.
2. Speak each vowel at a normal pace, still paying attention to how you use your mouth and lips. Continue for a minute or two.
3. Now tap the table for emphasis as you say each sound slowly, repeating the list.
4. Tap the table and say *a* three times.
5. Tap the table and say *e* three times.
6. Tap the table and say *i* three times.
7. Tap the table and say *o* three times.
8. Tap the table and say *u* three times.
9. Speak *a*, *e*, *i*, *o*, and *u* loudly for a few minutes.

Practice the vowels by combining them with a few consonants, as in the following chart. Start with the B row and repeat with the other rows.

- Speak the sounds in the row at a natural pace.
- Did they sound like the words below them? If so, good! If not, repeat the sounds until they do.
- Speak the sounds in the row at a quick pace three times.
- Speak the sounds in the row repeatedly.
- Change the sequence of the sounds in the row.

	A	E	I	O	U
B *sounds like*	Ba *bah*	Be *bay*	Bi *bee*	Bo *bow*	Bu *boo*
D *sounds like*	Da *dah*	De *day*	Di *dee*	Do *dough*	Du *do*
M *sounds like*	Ma *mah*	Me *may*	Mi *me*	Mo *mow*	Mu *moo*
T *sounds like*	Ta *tah*	Te *taint*	Ti *tea*	To *toe*	Tu *too*

Pronounce Spanish Consonants

Some consonants in Spanish have different sounds than they do in English.

Note: Bold syllables indicate where the natural emphasis falls.

Spanish letter	English sound	Spanish example
c (before *e* or *i*)	*s* as in *sit*	**cigarro** (see-**gah**-rroh)
g (before *e* or *i*)	*h* as in *hey*	**general** (heh-neh-**rahl**)
h	silent, like *k* in *knife*	**hombre** (**ohm**-bre)
j	*h* as in *hat*	**Julio** (**hoo**-lee-oh)
ll	*y* as in *yes*	**pollo** (**poh**-yoh)
ñ	*ny* as in *canyon*	**señor** (seh-**nyohr)**
q	*k* as in *kit*	**tequila** (teh-**kee**-lah)
rr	"rolled" *r* sound	**burro** (**boo**-rroh)
z	*s* as in *son*	**zapato** (sah-**pah**-toh)
v	*b* as in *boy*	**viento** (be-**ehn**-toe)

Directions

1. Read the letter and its description. Say the consonant sound.
2. Say the Spanish example.
3. Speak the example several times as you touch the word.
4. Say the example and touch the word.
5. Tap the example as you touch the word.
6. Repeat steps 1 to 4 for each letter in the table.
7. Speak each Spanish example five times.

Practice Spanish Pronunciation

Note: Bold syllables indicate where the natural emphasis falls.Directions

1. Read each of the following letter sections aloud.
2. Speak the example words.
3. Tap the example words.

C has two sounds.

Ca, *co*, and *cu* have a hard *k* sound, as in "cap."

- Cadera (*ka-**deh**-rah*) = hip
- Córnea (***kohr**-nay-ah*) = cornea
- Cúspide (***koos**-pee-day*) = cuspid, top
- Curar (***Ku**-rahr*) = to cure

Ci and *ce* have a soft *s* sound, like the *c* in "city."

- Cintura (*seen-**too**-rah*) = waist
- Celular (***say**-lou-lahr*) = cellular

G has two sounds.

Ga, *Go*, and *Gu* have a hard sound, as in "gap."

- Gástrico (***gahs**-tree-koh*) = gastric
- Gordo (***gore-**dough*) = fat
- Gota (***go**-tah*) = drop

Ge and *Gi* have a soft sound, like *h* in "hop."

- Germen (***hair**-men*) = germ
- Gigante (*he-**gahn**-tay*) = giant

H is the only silent consonant.

- Histeria (*eesss-**the**-reeh-ah*) = hysteria
- Hombro (***ohm**-broh*) = shoulder
- Hueso (***way**-so*) = bone

J is pronounced just like the soft Spanish *g* (i.e., like *h* in "hop").

- Jarabe (*ha-**rah**-bay*) = syrup
- Jeringa (*hey-**ring**-gah*) = syringe

Ll is considered a consonant in Spanish and sounds like the *y* in "yes."

- Nudillo (*new-**dee**-yoh*) = knuckle
- Llorar (***yoh**-rahr*) = to cry
- Llamaradas (*yah-mah-**rah**-dahs*) = hot flashes

Ñ sounds like the *ni* in onion or the *ny* in "canyon."

- Uña (***ooh**-nya*) = nail
- Uñero (*ooh-**nyeh**-roh*) = ingrown toenail
- Niño (***knee**-nyo*) = child
- Señor (***say**-nyor*) = sir, mister

Qu (**que** and **qui**) has a *k* sound.

- Quiste (***key**-stay*) = cyst
- Químico (***key**-mee-koh*) = chemical
- Quemado (kay-***mah***-dough) = burned
- Queja (***kay**-hah*) = complaint

Rr is very strongly trilled.

- Sarro (***sah**-roh*) = tartar of the teeth
- Cigarro (*see-**gar**-row*) = cigarette
- Carril (*car-**reehl***) = lane
- Ferrocarril (*fair-roh-car-**ril***) = railroad

Z is pronounced the same way as *c* before *e* or *i*, as in "sit."

- Zumbido (*zoom-**bee**-doh*) de los oídos = buzzing, humming in the ears
- Zambo (***sahm**-bow*) = knock-kneed
- Zurdo (***sewer**-doh*) = left-handed

The stressed syllable in Spanish words is often the next-to-last syllable. The rule is:

The natural stress falls on the next-to-last syllable of words ending in a vowel or in "n" or "s." For all other words, the natural stress falls on the last syllable.

The words in the following table change meaning when the stress changes. Study the word pairs as follows:

- Speak the word with its natural stress.
- Speak the word with the other stress.
- Repeat each pair six times.

Natural Stress	Other Stress
Esta (*this*) Esta niña (*this girl*) Esta doctora (*this doctor*)	**Está** (*he/she is, you are*) El está aquí. (*He is here.*) Ella está allí. (*She is there.*)
Hablo (*I speak*) Hablo con el paciente. (*I speak with the patient.*)	**Habló** (*he/she/you spoke*) Habló ayer con el. (*He spoke yesterday with him.*)
Camino (*I walk*) Camino diez minutos. (*I walk ten minutes.*)	**Caminó** (*he/she/you walked*) Caminó diez minutos. (*He/she/you walked ten minutes.*)
El estudio (*the study*) Está en el estudio. (*He is in the study.*) **Estudio** (*I study*) No estudio. (*I don't study.*)	**Estudió** (*He/she/you studied*) Estudió por una hora. (*He/she/you studied for an hour.*)
El ano (*the anus*) Tiene que examinar el ano. (*He has to examine the anus.*)	**El año** (*the year*) Favor de regresar el proximo año. (*Please return next year.*)

Start a Conversation

Introduce Yourself

Introduce yourself with:

- **Me llamo** ________________. (I call myself _______.)

Ask the patient his or her name:

- **¿Cómo te llamas?** (Familiar "you" form: use with a child.)

- **¿Cómo se llama (usted)?** (Formal "you" form: use to express respect.)

The patient replies with one of the following:

- **Mi nombre es** ________________ (My name is _______.)
- **Mi apellido es** ________________ (My last name is _______.)
- **Mi apodo es** ________________ (My nickname is _______.)

Pleasure to Meet You

Complete the introduction:

- **Mucho gusto.** *Much pleasure.*

Your patient replies with one of the following:

- **El gusto es mío.** *The pleasure is mine.*
- **Igualmente.** *Equally.*
- **Encantado.** *Enchanted*, he says.
- **Encantada.** *Enchanted*, she says.

How Old Are You?—¿Cuántos Años Tiene?

You sometimes ask your patient, "How old are you?" In Spanish the question is, "How many years do you have?"

When speaking with your boss, your teacher, or an adult patient, you will use the formal (usted) form of respect.

To express respect, use the formal form: *tiene*.
¿Cuántos años tiene usted?

To express closeness, or with children, adolescents, or your friend, you will use the familiar (tú) form: *tienes*.
¿Cuántos años tienes? or **¿Cuántos años tienes tú?**

Patients answer with: **Tengo ______ años.**
I have ______ years.

Practice

1. Ask the formal question twice. Stand up and ask it twice. Walk a step and ask it twice. Tap it twice.
2. Repeat the same practice with the familiar question.
3. Ask a girl her age and give the "cinco" answer. Repeat for each answer. Stand up and tap this practice.
4. Ask a man his age and give the "treinta" answer. Repeat for each answer. Stand up and tap this practice.

Question	Answer	
¿Cuántos años tiene? *Formal*	**Tengo cinco años.** I have five years.	**Tengo treinta años.** I have thirty years.
¿Cuántos años tienes? *Familiar*	**Tengo once años.** I have eleven years.	**Tengo cincuenta y dos años.** I have fifty-two years.
	Tengo dieciseis años. I have sixteen years.	**Tengo setenta años.** I have seventy years.

How Are You?—¿Cómo Está?

You often ask your patient, "How are you?"

To express respect, use the formal form: *está*.
¿Cómo está? or **¿Cómo está usted?**

To express closeness or with children or adolescents, use the familiar form: *estás*.
¿Cómo estás?

Patients answer with: **Estóy ______**
I am, understood as "I feel"

Practice

1. Ask the formal question twice. Stand up and ask it twice. Walk a step and ask it twice. Tap it twice.
2. Repeat the same practice with the familiar question.
3. Study the meaning of each answer in the following table.
4. Repeat the question practice steps for each answer.
5. Ask a boy how he feels and give the "well" answer. Repeat for each answer. Stand up and tap this practice.
6. Ask a woman how she feels and give the "well" answer. Repeat for each answer. Stand up and tap this practice.

Question	Answer
¿Cómo está? *Formal:* How are you? **¿Cómo estás?** *Familiar:* How are you?	**Estoy bien.** I am well. **Estoy mal.** I am bad. **Estoy regular.** I am okay. **Estoy así así.** I am so-so. **Estoy contento/a.** I feel happy. **Estoy alegre.** I feel happy.

Chapter 3: Pain and Medical Objects

Communicate about Pain

Identifying Body Parts—Words to Learn

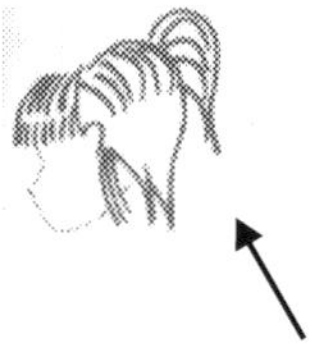 Hair = **El pelo**	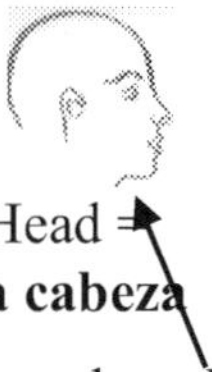 Head = **La cabeza** The neck = **el cuello**	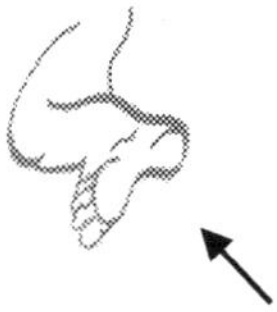 Foot = **El pie** Sole = **la planta del pie**	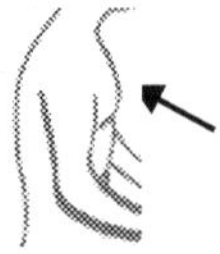 Chest = **El pecho**
 Mouth = **La boca** Lips = **Los labios**	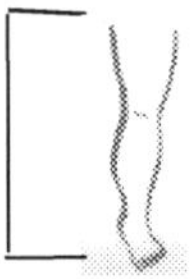 Leg = **La pierna**	 Hand = **La mano**	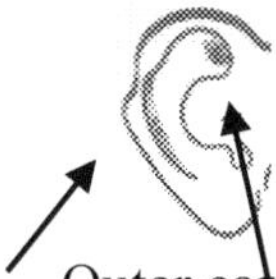 Outer ear = **La oreja** Inner ear = **El oído**
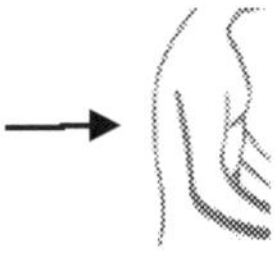 Back = **La espalda**	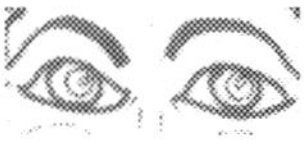 Eyes = **Los ojos**	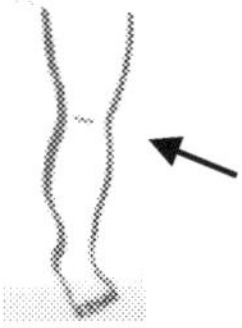 Knee = **La rodilla**	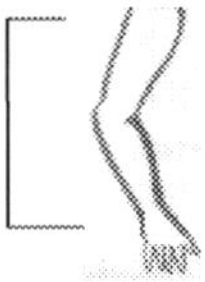 Arm = **El brazo**
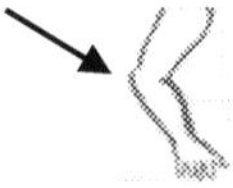 Elbow **El codo**	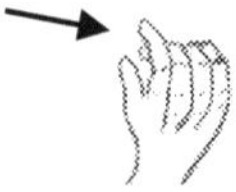 Finger = **El dedo**	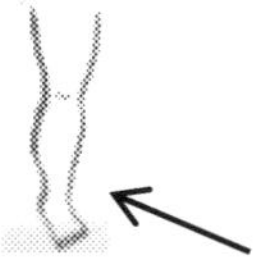 Ankle = **El tobillo**	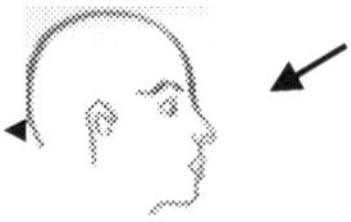 Nose = **La nariz**

Body Parts—Practice

1. Touch each body part picture and speak its Spanish name.
2. Touch each body part picture and tap its Spanish name.
3. Touch each body part on yourself, and speak its Spanish name three times.

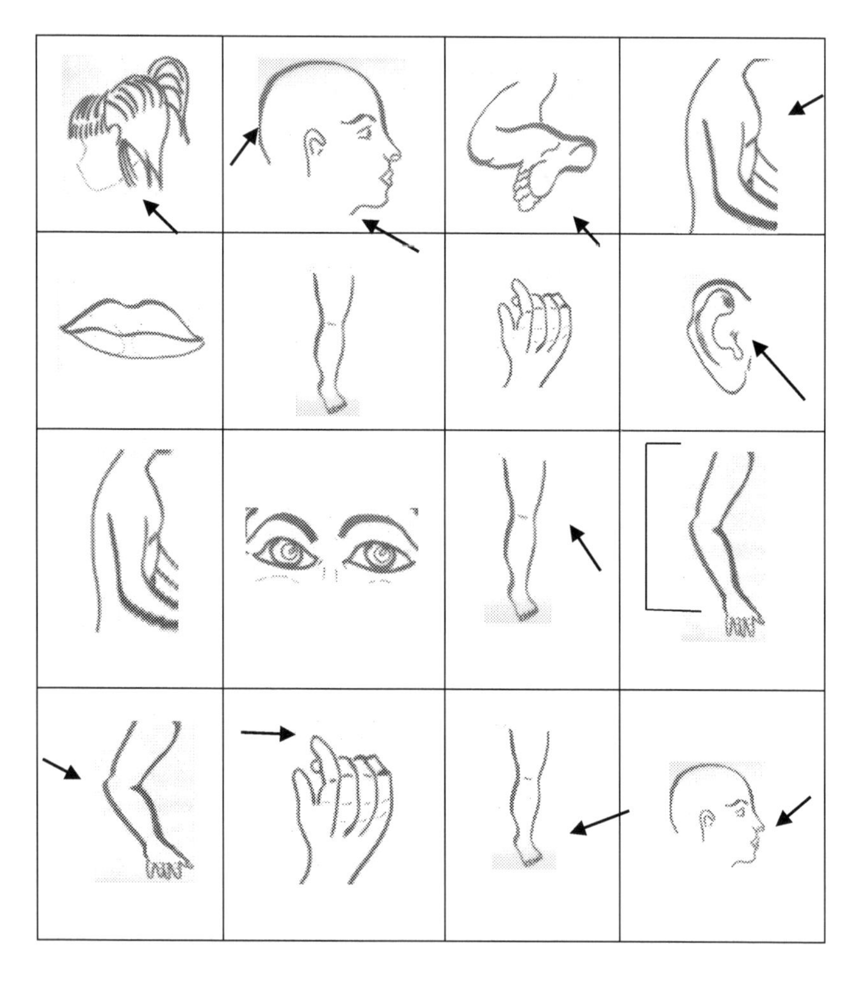

Word Bank: la espalda, el brazo, la nariz, el puño, la mano, el oído, la pierna, el pelo, los labios, la boca, el codo, la oreja, el tobillo, la planta del pie, la rodilla, el dedo, el cuello

Body Parts That Hurt—Doler

To express pain in Spanish, use *doler* (to hurt).

To communicate pain that **you** feel, you say:

Me	**duele**	[body part in Spanish].
Me	it hurts	[the body part].

To communicate pain that **he or she** feels, you say:

Le	**duele**	[body part in Spanish].
Him or her	it hurts	[the body part].

To ask about pain **someone else** feels, raise your tone at the end.

¿Le duele?
*Are **you** hurting? Is **she** or **he** hurting?*

Or

¿Qué	**le**	**duele?**
What	*to you*	*is hurting?*
What	*to him/her*	*is hurting?*

Study the pattern for using *doler* in the following table.

- "**Me duele** [body part]" or "**Le duele** [body part]"
- "**Me duelen** [body parts]" or "**Le duelen** [body parts]"

Spanish	English
Me duele la cabeza.	*Literal translation:* The head is hurting me. *Actual translation*: My head hurts.
Le duele la cabeza.	*Literal translation:* The head is hurting him/her/you. *Actual translation*: His/her/your head hurts.
Me duele**n** los ojos.	*Literal translation:* The eyes are hurting me. *Actual translation:* My eyes hurt.
Le duele**n** los ojos.	*Literal translation:* The eyes are hurting him/her/you. *Actual translation:* His/her/your eyes hurt.

Important: Many other verbs use the same pattern as doler (to hurt). Expand your communication by referring to this site: http://www.studyspanish.com/lessons/gustar.htm

Practice the pattern for using *doler* with the pictures below.

1. Touch each picture and say, "**Me duele** [body part]." Repeat.
2. Touch each picture and tap, "**Me duele** [body part]." Repeat.
3. Touch the body part on yourself and say, "**Me duele** [body part]."
4. Touch the body part on yourself and tap, "**Me duele** [body part]."
5. Touch each picture and ask, "**¿Le duele** [body part]?" Repeat.
6. Touch each picture and tap, "**¿Le duele** [body part]?" Repeat.
7. Touch the body part on yourself and tap, "**¿Le duele** [body part]?"

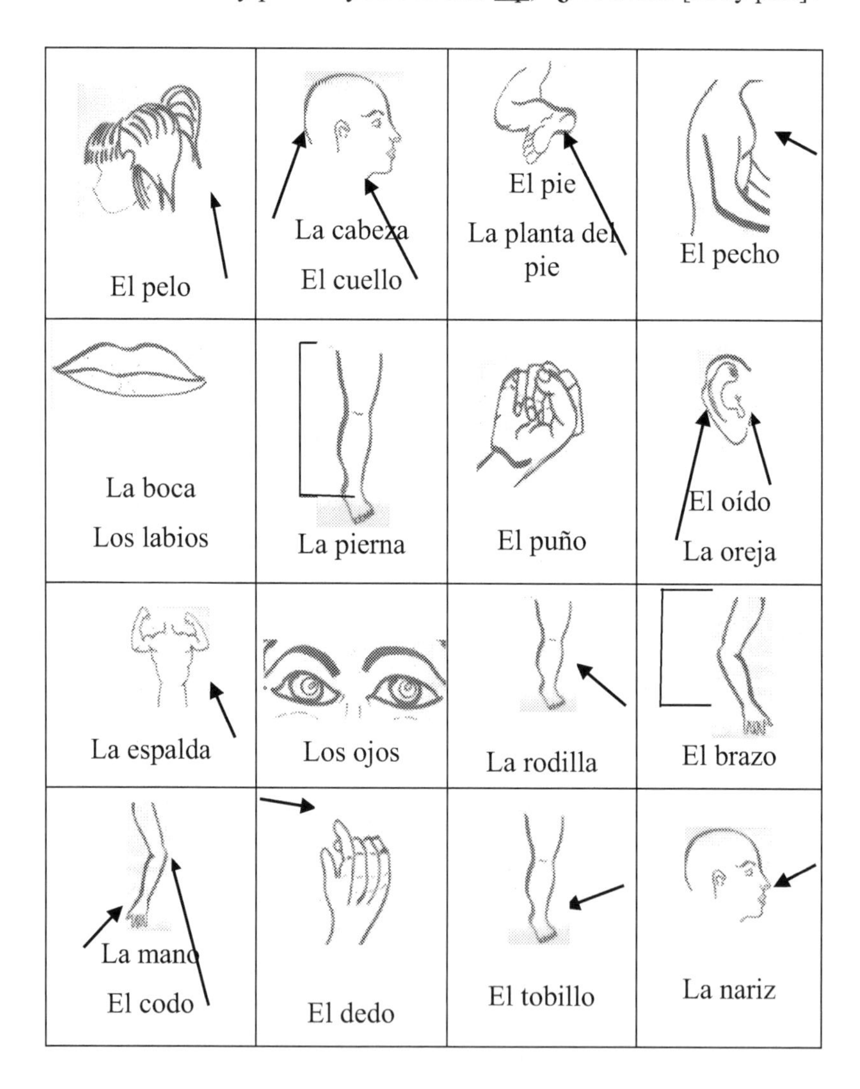

Body Parts That Hurt (Doler)—Practice

To ask, "Where does it hurt?" say:

¿Dónde	le	duele?
Where	*to you*	*is hurting?*

Practice using *doler* in a short conversation about the body parts you have learned. For each picture in the following table, (1) speak as the medical practitioner and then (2) answer as the patient.

As the medical practitioner, ask:	As the patient, answer:
¿Dónde le duele?	**Me duele** [body part]. Or **Me duelen** [body parts].

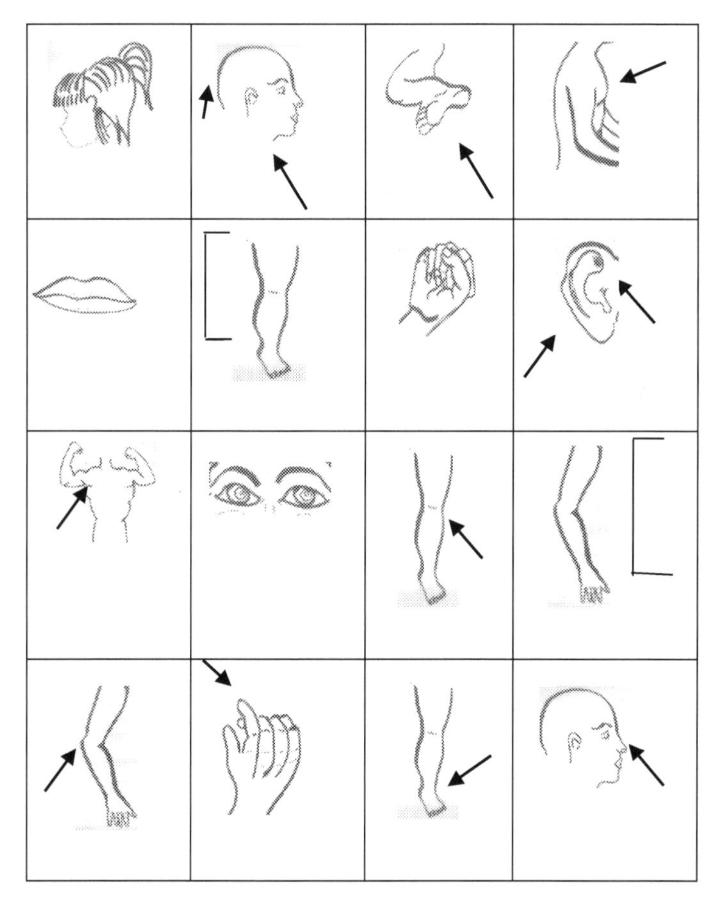

Word Bank: la espalda, el brazo, la nariz, el puño, la mano, el oído, la pierna, el pelo, los labios, la boca, el codo, la oreja, el tobillo, la planta del pie, la rodilla, el dedo, la cabeza, el cuello

Body Parts That Have Pain—Tener Dolor
Express pain in Spanish with *tener dolor* (to have pain).

To communicate pain that **you yourself (I)** have, say:

Tengo	**dolor de (en)**	la/las/el/los [body part].
I have	*pain of (in)*	*the [body part/parts].*

To communicate pain that **he or she** has, say:

Tiene	**dolor de**	la/las/el/los [body part].
He/she has	*pain of*	*the [body part/parts].*
Usted (you) have	*pain of*	*the [body part/parts].*

Notice the pattern in the following table for using "tener dolor."

- **Tengo dolor de** [feminine body part or plural body parts]
- **Tiene dolor del (de + el)** [masculine body part]

Spanish	English
Tengo dolor del pecho.	I have pain of the chest.
Tiene dolor del pecho.	You, he, or she has pain of the chest.
Tengo dolor en las manos.	I have pain in the hands.
Tiene dolor en las manos.	You, he, or she has pain in the hands.

Learn to use the "tener dolor" pattern using the following table.

1. Touch each picture and say, "**Tengo dolor de** [the body part]."
2. Touch each picture and tap, "**Tengo dolor de** [the body part]."
3. Touch the part on your body and say, "**Tengo dolor de** [body part]."
4. Touch the part on your body and tap, "**Tengo dolor de** [body part]."
5. Touch each picture and ask, "**¿Tiene dolor de** [the body part]?"
6. Touch the part on your body and tap, "**¿Tiene dolor de** [the body part)?"

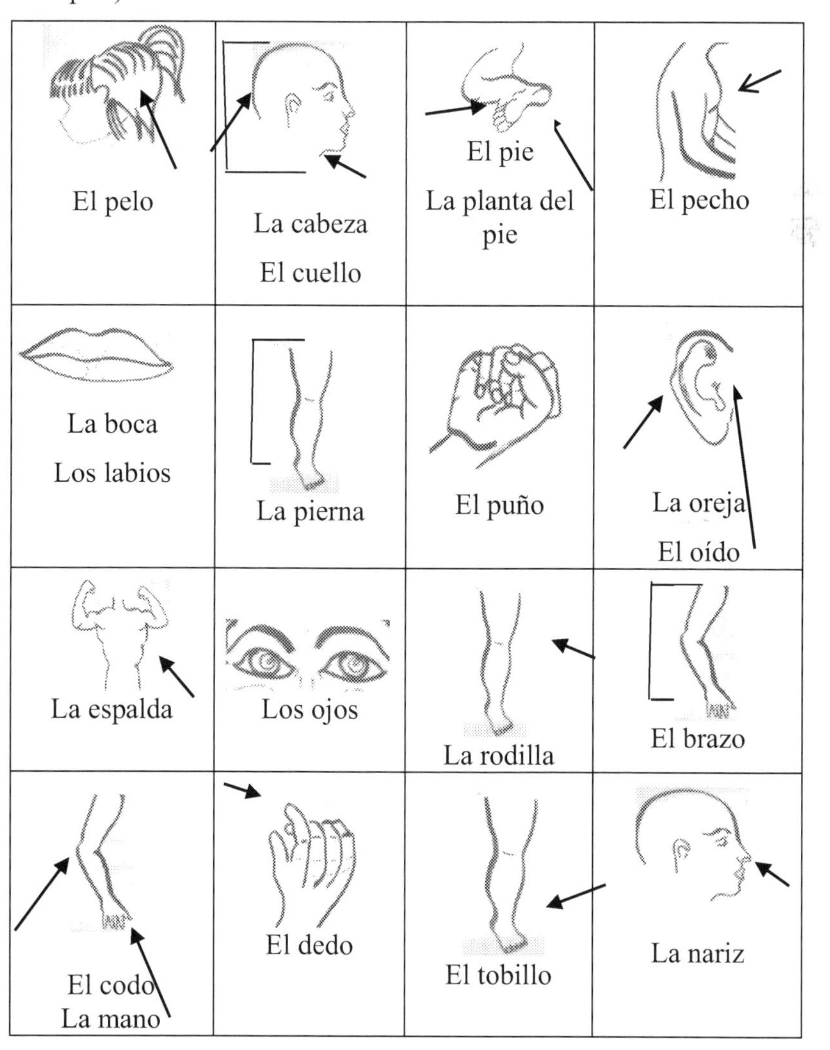

El pelo	La cabeza El cuello	El pie La planta del pie	El pecho
La boca Los labios	La pierna	El puño	La oreja El oído
La espalda	Los ojos	La rodilla	El brazo
El codo La mano	El dedo	El tobillo	La nariz

Do You Have Pain?—¿Le Duele? ¿Tiene Dolor de?

Ask patients if they have pain with the questions in the following table.

1. Study the table content.
2. Ask each question and give an answer from the Answer column.
3. Repeat each answer twice.
4. Practice the question with each answer.
5. Practice "¿Dónde tiene dolor?" with the answers in the next table, titled "Where Is Your Pain?"

Question	Answer
¿Le duele ahora? Is it hurting you now?	**¡Sí!** Yes! **¡Sí, tengo dolor!** Yes, I have pain! **¡Sí, tiene dolor!** Yes, she/he has pain! **¡Sí, mucho dolor!** Yes, much pain!
¿Tiene dolor? Do you have pain? Does she/he have pain?	
¿Dónde tiene dolor? Where do you have pain? Where does she/he have pain?	**Tengo dolor de** … I have pain of …
¿Tiene dolor de (la) cabeza? Do you have pain of the head?	**¡Sí, tengo dolor de (la) cabeza!** Yes, I have pain of the head (i.e., a headache).
¿Tiene dolor de (los) ojos? Do you have pain of the eyes?	**¡Sí, tengo dolor de (los) ojos!** Yes, I have pain of the eyes.

Note: Using the article (el, la, los, las) is optional.

Where Is Your Pain?—¿Dónde le Duele?

Ask patients to show you the *location* of their pain.

1. For each body part, speak the "mostrar" request and the answer. **Mostrar** means "to show."
2. Repeat while you point to the same body part on your body.
3. In the table, tap the "mostrar" request. Then answer by pointing to the body part on yourself.
4. Follow steps 1 to 3 for "tocar." **Tocar** means "to touch.

Request	Answer			
Favor de mostrar dónde le duele. Do me the favor of showing where it hurts. **Favor de tocar dónde le duele.** Do me the favor of touching where it hurts.	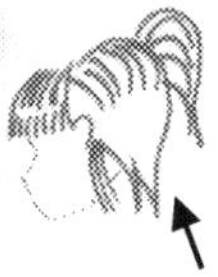 El pelo	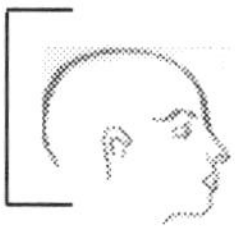 La cabeza	 El pie	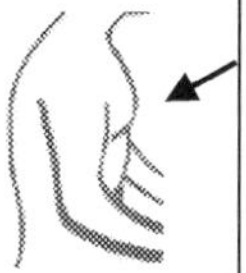 El pecho
	 La boca, Los labios	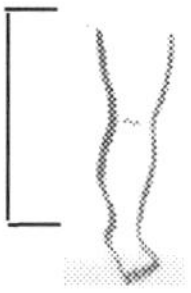 La pierna	 El puño	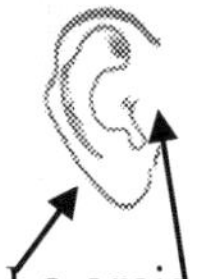 La oreja El oído
	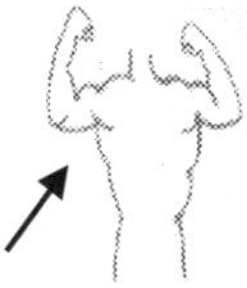 La espalda	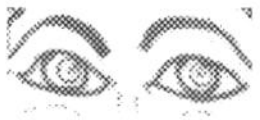 Los ojos	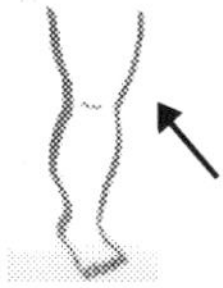 La rodilla	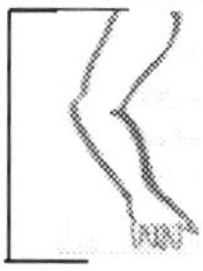 El brazo
	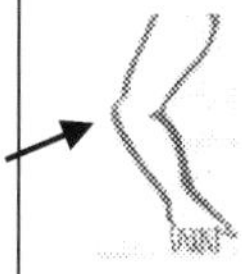 El codo	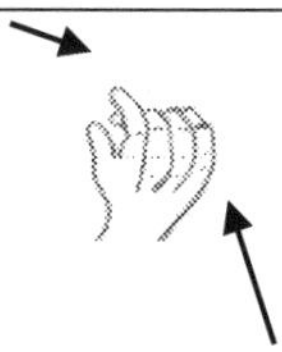 El dedo La mano	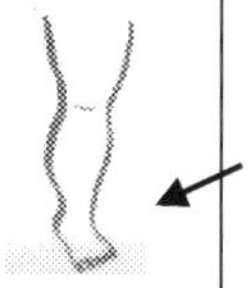 El tobillo	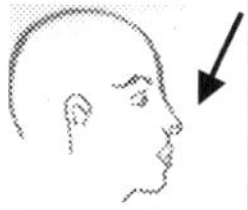 La nariz

How Much Pain Do You Have?—¿Cuánto Dolor Tiene?

Ask patients to show you the *level* of their pain.

1. Study the following table content. Practice the request with each answer.
2. Speak the request and an answer from the Answer column.
3. Point to the degree-of-pain face on the scale at the bottom of the table as you say the associated phrase.
4. Repeat each answer twice.

<table>
<tr><th colspan="5">Request</th><th colspan="5">Answer</th></tr>
<tr><td colspan="5">Favor de señalar
al número que indica
el nivel del dolor.

Please point out
the number that indicates
the level of pain.</td><td colspan="5">1—sin dolor
without pain
2—dolor muy leve
very mild pain
3—dolor leve
mild pain
4—dolor muy moderado
very moderate pain
5—dolor moderado
moderate pain
6—dolor fuerte
strong pain
7—dolor severo
severe pain
9—dolor muy severo
very severe pain
10—dolor intolerable
intolerable pain</td></tr>
<tr><td></td><td></td><td></td><td></td><td></td><td></td><td></td><td></td><td></td><td></td></tr>
<tr><td>1</td><td>2</td><td>3</td><td>4</td><td>5</td><td>6</td><td>7</td><td>8</td><td>9</td><td>10</td></tr>
</table>

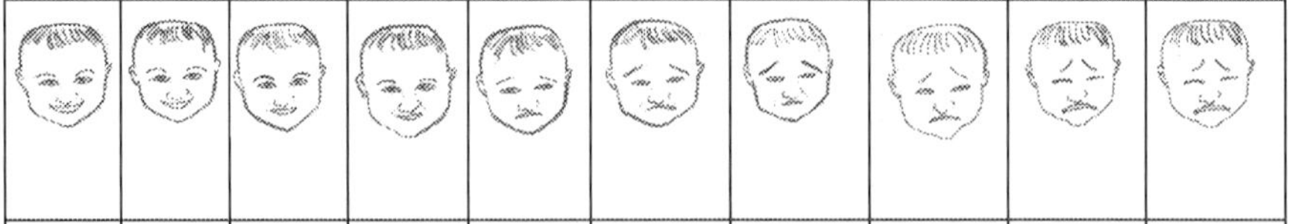

Tell Me about the Pain—¿Cómo Es el Dolor?

You often ask patients to *describe* their pain.

Question–Answer Tables

Practice each question with each answer provided in the following tables.

1. Ask each question in the Question column and give one answer from the Answer column.
2. Stand up and repeat the question with each answer twice.
3. Sit down and tap the question with each answer twice.

Question	Answer
¿Cuánto tiempo hace que tiene el dolor? How long does it make that you have the pain? *Note: In English we would ask, "How long have you had this pain?"*	**Semana y media.** A week and a half. **Cuatro días.** Four days. **Ayer.** Yesterday. **Anoche, las dos.** Last night, two o'clock. **Esta mañana.** This morning.
¿Cuándo es mayor? When is it greater?	**De noche.** At night. **De día.** At day.

Question	Answer
¿Cómo es el dolor? How is the pain?	**Constante.** Constant. **Va y viene.** It goes and comes. **Se va y se le quita.** It goes and it stops.

Beginning–Question End–Answer Table

Practice each possible question in the following table, and answer each question with each possible answer.

1. Begin each question with "¿Es el dolor?" and use a phrase in the Question End column.
2. Give one answer from the Answer column.
3. Stand up and repeat the question with each answer twice.
4. Sit down and tap the question with each answer twice.
5. Repeat steps 1 to 4 for each phrase in the Question End column and each answer in the Answer column.

Beginning	Question End	Answer
¿Es el dolor …	**Fuerte o leve?** Strong or light?	**Fuerte.** Strong. **Leve.** Light.
	Sordo o agudo? Dull or sharp?	**Sordo.** Dull. **Agudo.** Sharp.
	Continuo? Steady? **Todo el tiempo?** All the time? **Ardiente?** Burning? **Sensación de presión?** Feeling of pressure? **Calambre?** Cramp? **Palpitante?** Throbbing? **Aplastante?** Crushing?	**Sí.** Yes. **No.** No.

Communicate about Medical Objects

Object Names Are Masculine or Feminine

Nouns in Spanish have gender; they are *masculine or feminine.*

- **El** before the noun indicates masculine.
- **La** indicates feminine.

Most words for a man end in "o" because they are masculine words.
Most words for a woman end in "a" because they are feminine words.

El (*masculine*)	**La (*feminine*)**
el médico, **el doctor** (the male doctor)	**la doctora** (the female doctor)
el técnico (the male technician)	**la técnica** (the female technician)
el enfermero (the male nurse)	**la enfermera** (the female nurse)
el dentista (the male dentist)	**la dentista** (the female dentist)

Describing words, such as colors, match the noun's gender and number. Here are a few examples.

Feminine Singular	**Feminine Plural**
la bata roja	las batas rojas
la mano pequeña	las manos pequeñas

Masculine Singular	**Masculine Plural**
el camisón rojo	los camisones rojos
el termómetro grande	los termómetros grandes

Identify Medical Objects
When you talk to patients, you often ask them to wear something, take off something, sit, or lie on objects. You also identify objects used to examine or treat them.

Medical Objects—Words to Learn

Learn the words for each object in the following table.

1. Touch each picture and speak its Spanish name.
2. Stand up, touch each picture, and speak its Spanish name.
3. Sit down, touch each picture, and tap its Spanish name.

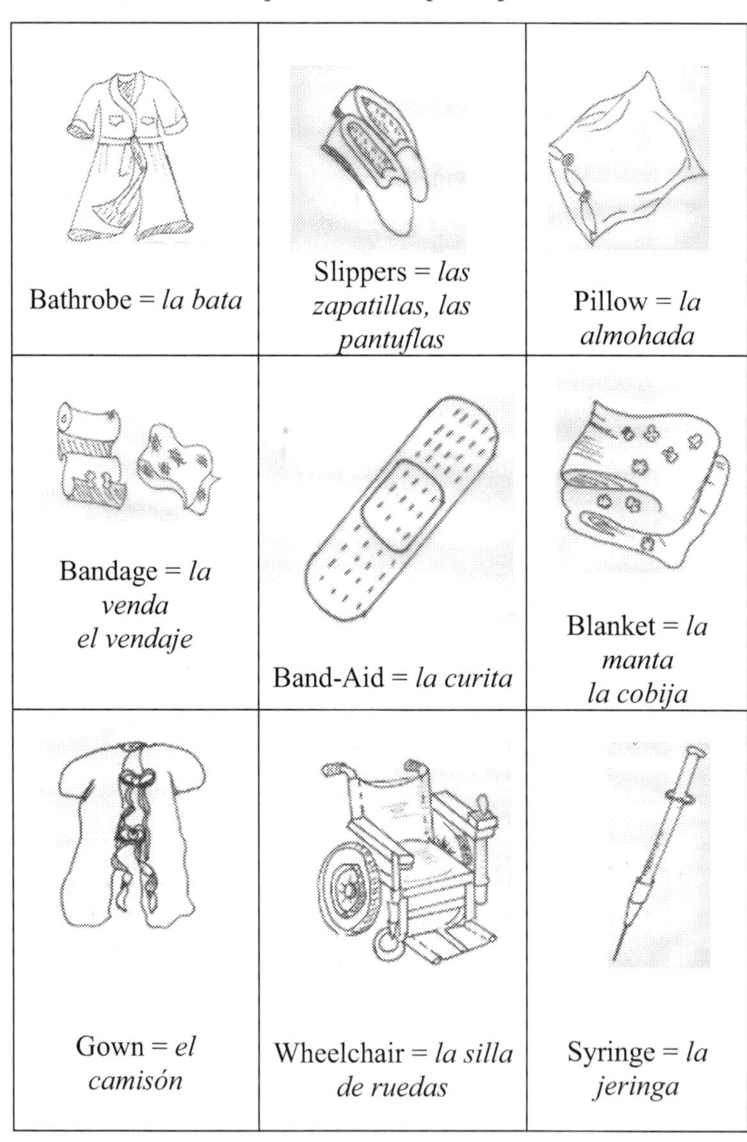

Bathrobe = *la bata*	Slippers = *las zapatillas, las pantuflas*	Pillow = *la almohada*
Bandage = *la venda el vendaje*	Band-Aid = *la curita*	Blanket = *la manta la cobija*
Gown = *el camisón*	Wheelchair = *la silla de ruedas*	Syringe = *la jeringa*

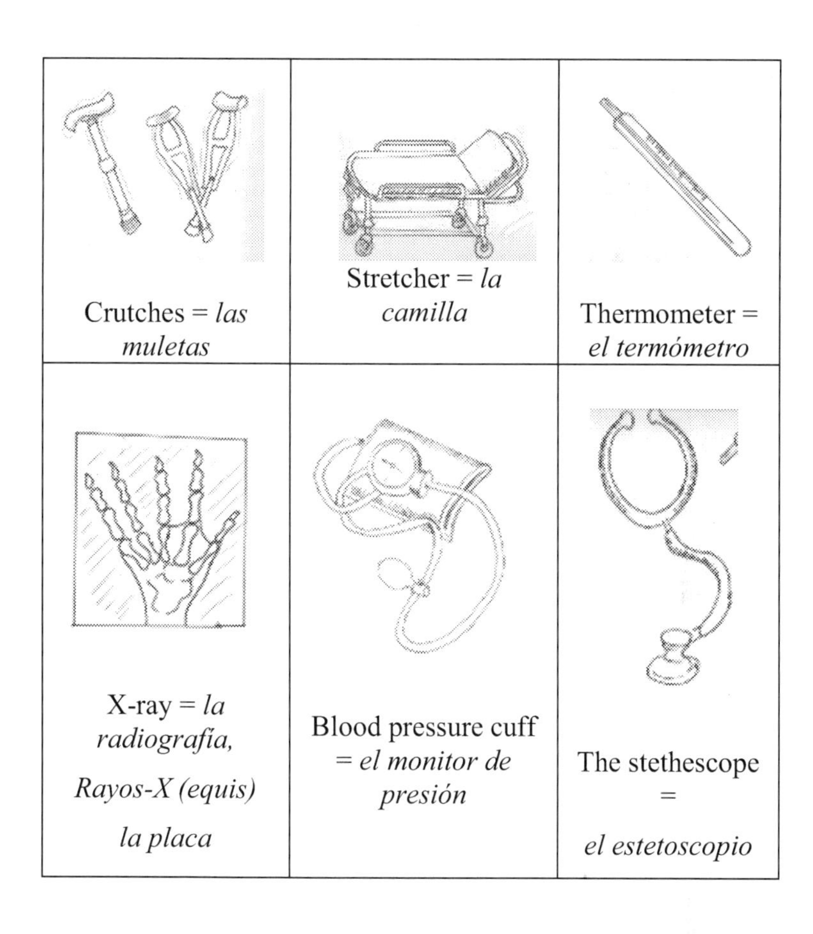

Crutches = *las muletas*	Stretcher = *la camilla*	Thermometer = *el termómetro*
X-ray = *la radiografía,* *Rayos-X (equis)* *la placa*	Blood pressure cuff = *el monitor de presión*	The stethescope = *el estetoscopio*

Medical Objects—Practice

1. For each row, touch each object and speak its Spanish name slowly three times. Then speak it quickly, twice.
2. For each column, do the same.
3. Touch the objects randomly, tapping their Spanish names

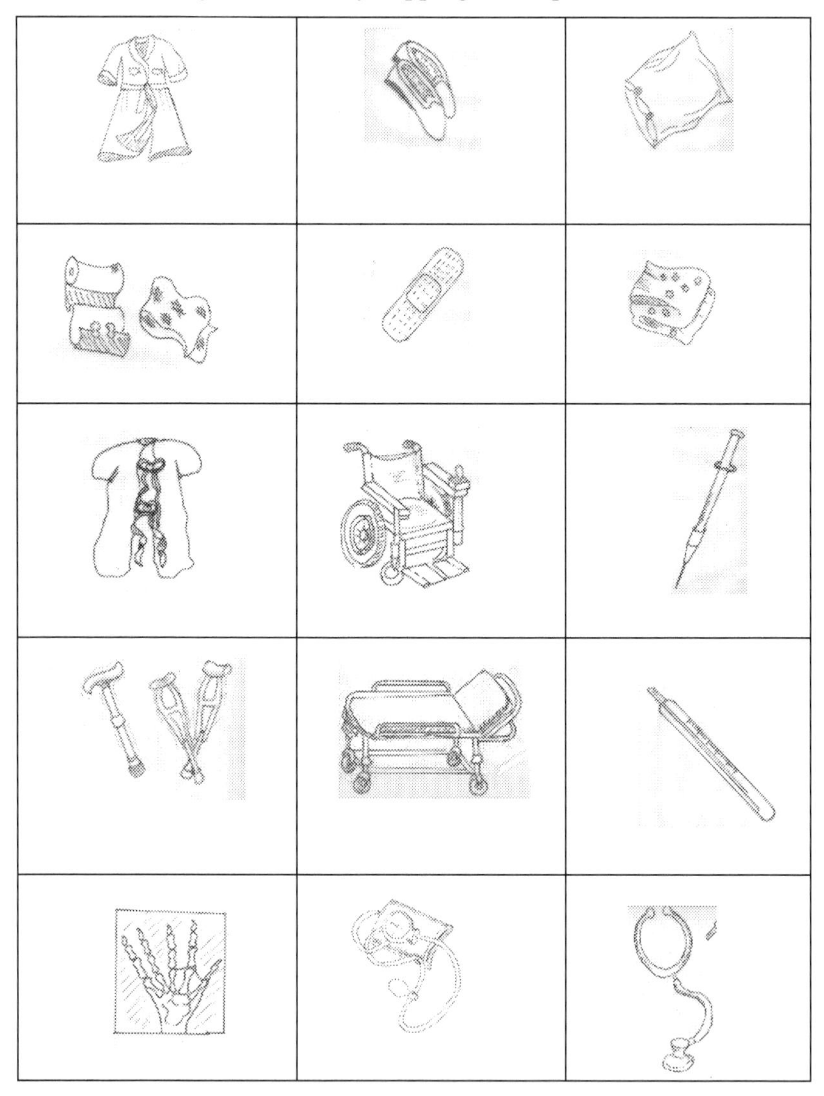

Word Bank: el vendaje, la bata, el estetoscopio, las pantuflas, el camisón, la almohada, la radiografía, el monitor de presión, la venda, la manta, las zapatillas, la silla con ruedas, la curita, la jeringa, las muletas, la camilla, el termómetro

Do You Have That Medical Object?—Tener

You will sometimes ask other medical staff or patients whether they have an object used to examine or take care of patients.

The action word for "to have" is *tener*.
When you ask if someone has something, *tener* becomes *tiene*.

¿Tiene? = Do you have? / Does she have? / Does he have?

Question: **¿Tiene _____?** Do you have ____?

Answer: **¡Sí, lo tengo/la tengo!** Yes, I have it/one.

The answer can be:

- **Sí.** (Yes.)
- **No.** (No.)
- **Sí, tengo** [the object in the question]. (Yes, I have the object.)
- **No, no tengo** [the object in the question]. (No, I do not have the object.)

Example: **¿Tiene la bata? ¡Si, tengo la bata! ¡No tengo la bata!**

Answers often omit the object name and instead include the pronoun—*la*, *las*, *lo*, or *los*—to match the objects asked about. The object is understood.

Example: **¿Tiene una manta? ¡Si, la tengo! ¡No, no la tengo!**

In the following table, each row is an example question with answers.

1. Ask each question and give its yes answer.
2. Stand up and repeat.
3. Tap each question and its yes answer.
4. Repeat steps 1 to 3 with the no answers.

Question	Answer	
	Yes …	No …
¿Tiene la bata?	Sí, la tengo.	No, no la tengo.
¿Tiene las muletas?	Sí, las tengo.	No, no las tengo.
¿Tiene el rayo-X?	Sí, lo tengo.	No, no lo tengo.
¿Tiene los rayos-X?	Sí, los tengo.	No, no los tengo.

Do You Have That Medical Object?—Practice Tener

Practice asking for medical objects and saying whether you have them.

1. For each row, touch each object and ask, "Tiene _____?" Answer that yes, you have each object/objects.
2. Repeat each question and answer that no, you do not have the object.
3. Repeat steps 1 and 2 for the objects in each column.

 la bata	 las zapatillas/ pantuflas	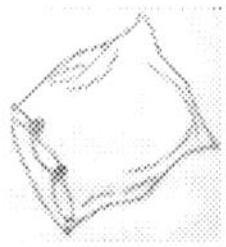 la almohada
 las vendas, los vendajes	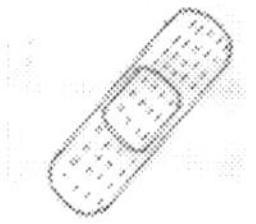 la curita	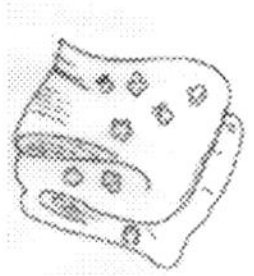 la manta
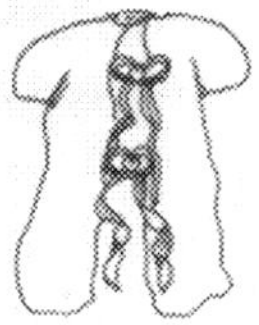 el camisón	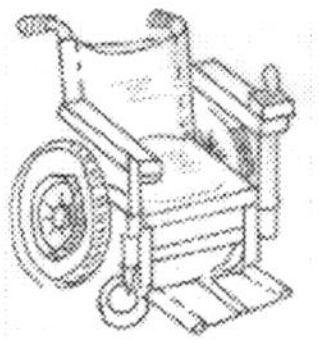 la silla de ruedas	 la jeringa
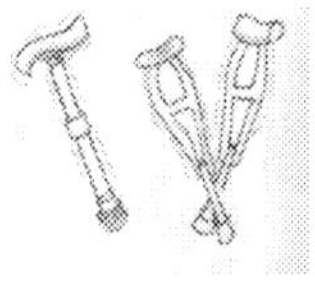 las muletas	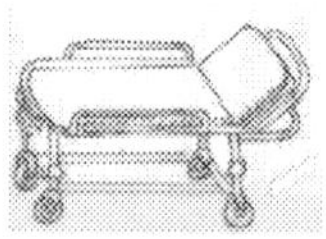 la camilla	 el termómetro
 la radiografía, el X-rayo	 el monitor de presión (arterial)	 un estetescopio

Is There a Medical Object?—¿Hay?

To ask if a medical object is available: **¿Hay _____?**
To answer: **¡Sí, hay!** or **¡No, no hay!**

Each row in the following table has a question with the yes and no answers. Notice that the answers do not name the object asked for.

Question	Answer	
¿Hay una bata?	Sí, hay.	No, no hay.
¿Hay muletas?	Sí, hay.	No, no hay.
¿Hay un rayo-X?	Sí, hay.	No, no hay.
¿Hay unos rayos X?	Sí, hay.	No, no hay.

Practice asking if medical objects are available using the following table.

1. Ask if each object is available and answer yes.
2. Ask if each object is available and answer no.
3. Tap and repeat steps 1 and 2.

una bata	unas zapatillas/ pantuflas	una almohada	unas muletas	una radiografía, un rayo-X
unas vendas, unos vendajes	una silla de ruedas	*blanket* una manta	una camilla	un monitor de presión (arterial)
un camisón	una curita	una jeringa	un termómetro	un estetoscopio

Where Is That Object?—¿Dónde Está?

To ask for the location of an object, say, "¿Dónde está?"
To answer, state the location of the object.

In the diagrams below, each Spanish word or phrase states the location of a ball relative to a line, another ball, or a box.

1. Ask, "**¿Dónde está?**" and speak each location, touching its ball.
2. Stand and repeat step 1. Sit and repeat step 1, tapping all words.

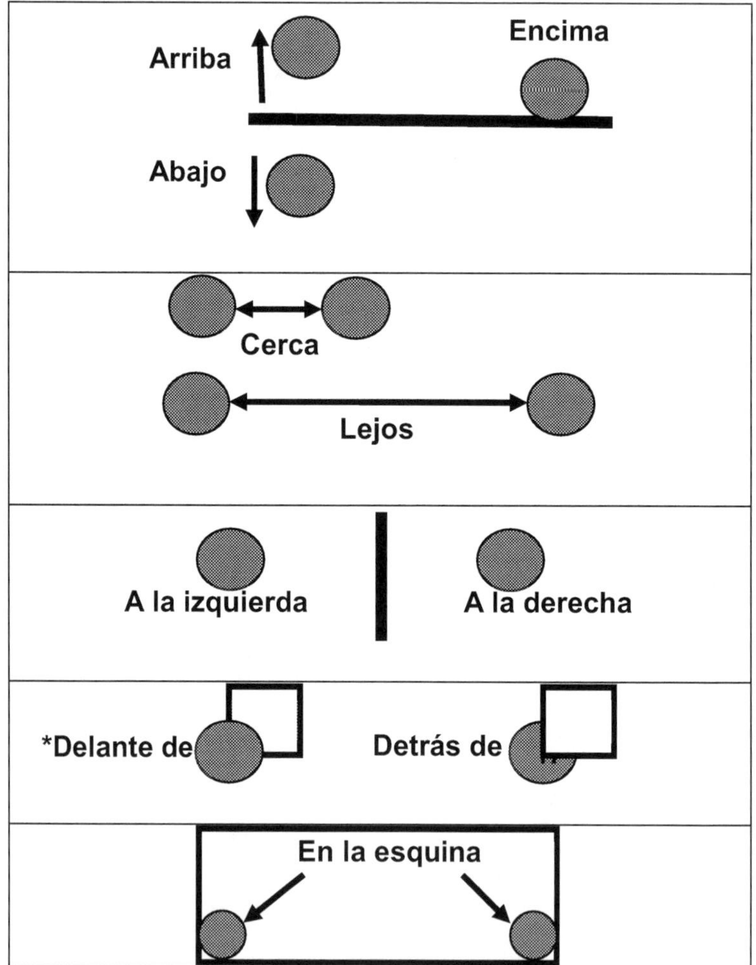

*"Enfrente de" means "in front of and facing."

Practice the locations in Spanish again.

1. Touch each ball in the following picture and say its location word or phrase.
2. Stand up and repeat. Sit down and repeat. Repeat tapping the words.

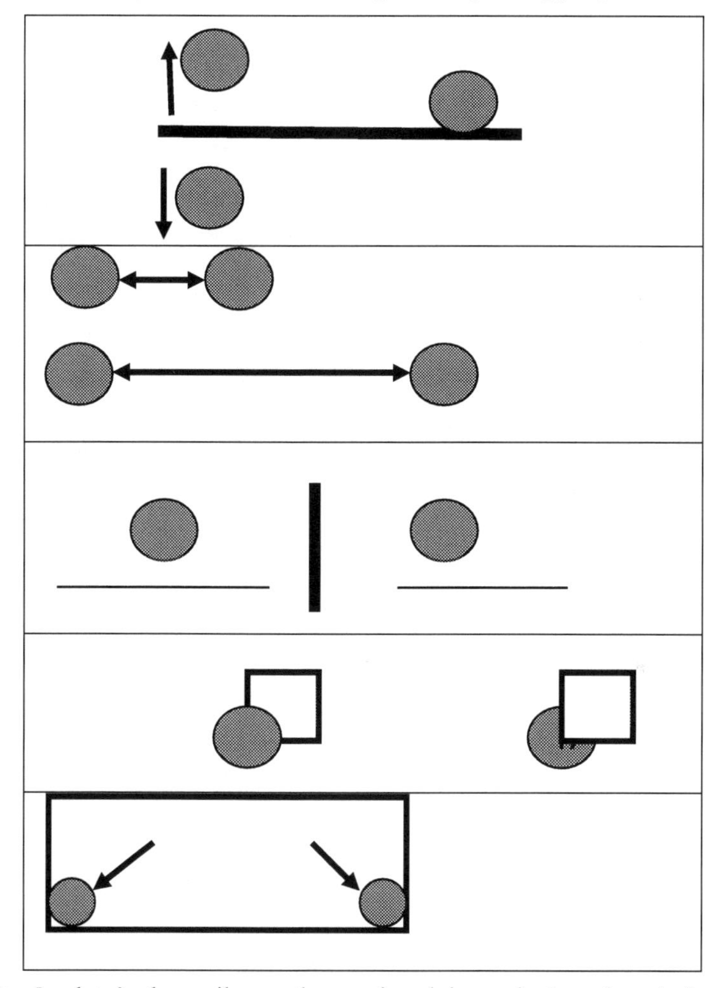

Word Bank: detrás de, arriba, en la esquina, lejos, a la derecha, abajo, delante de, encima, a la izquierda, detrás de, derecho, cerca

To ask where a medical object is located, say, "¿Dónde está/están _____?"
To answer, say, "Está/Están __________."

1. Ask the location of each object in the following pictures.
2. Answer with its location relative to another object in the square.

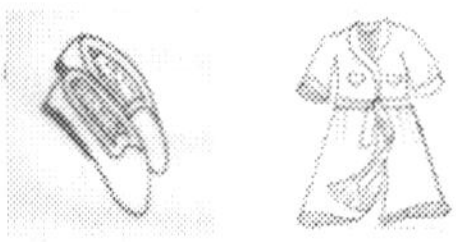	¿Dónde está la bata? Está a derecha de las pantuflas. ¿Dónde están las pantuflas? Están a la la izquierda del camisón.
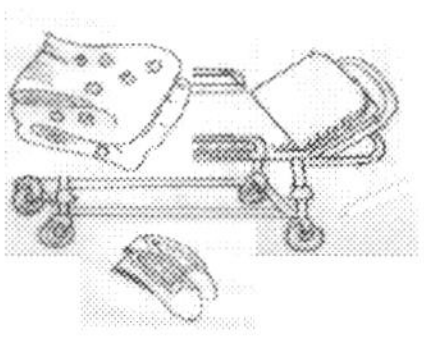	¿Dónde está la manta? Está encima de la camilla. ¿Dónde está la camilla? Está arriba de las zapatillas. ¿Dónde están las zapatillas? Están abajo de la camilla.
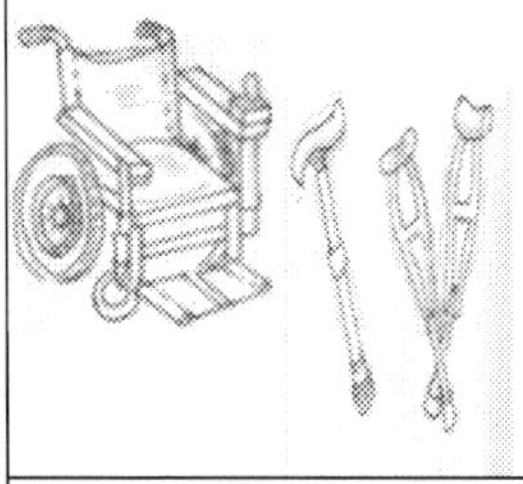	¿Dónde está la silla de ruedas? Está cerca de las muletas. Está a la izquierda de las muletas. ¿Dónde están las muletas? Están cerca de la silla de ruedas. Están a la derecha de la silla de ruedas.
	¿Dónde está la curita? Está lejos del termómetro. ¿Dónde está el termómetro? Está cerca de las vendas. ¿Dónde están las vendas? Están cerca del termómetro.
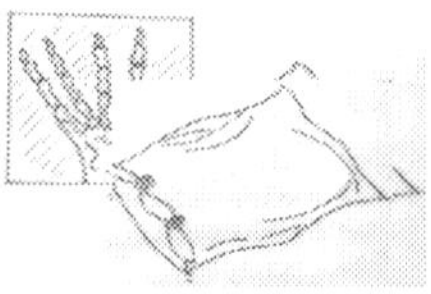	¿Dónde está la radiografía? Está detrás de la almohada. ¿Dónde está la almohada? Está delante de la radiografía.

3. Ask the location of each object in the following pictures.
4. Answer with its location relative to another object in the square.

	¿Dónde está el camisón? ______________________________ ¿Dónde están las pantuflas? ______________________________
	¿Dónde está la manta? ______________________________ ¿Dónde está la camilla? ______________________________ ¿Dónde están las zapatillas? ______________________________
	¿Dónde está la silla de ruedas? ______________________________ ¿Dónde están las muletas? ______________________________
	¿Dónde está la curita? ______________________________ ¿Dónde está el termómetro? ______________________________ ¿Dónde están las vendas? ______________________________
	¿Dónde está la radiografía? ______________________________ ¿Dónde está la almohada? ______________________________

Word Bank

atrás = behind	**delante de** = in front of
encima = on top of	**abajo** = below
arriba = above	**detrás de** = in back of
a la izquierda = to the left	**a la derecha** = to the right
cerca = near	**lejos** = far
en la esquina = in the corner	**derecho** = straight ahead

Chapter 4: Mix-and-Match Sentence Tables

How to Use the Mix-and-Match Tables

The three-part tables in this chapter for the mix-and-match method always have "Beginning," "Action Word," and "Ending" columns.

To say what you want to say:

1. Choose a word or phrase from the Beginning column.
2. Choose the action word from the Action Word column.
3. Choose an ending from the Ending column *if* it is needed to state your message.

The phrases in the Beginning column are used in most three-part tables. Always use a beginning phrase to start each sentence.

The phrases in the other two columns are the focus of the lesson. Always use an action word phrase. Use an ending phrase if it makes sense in your communication.

Example sentences from following table:

- Favor de + abrir + la boca.
- Es importante + levantarse. (*An ending word is not used here.*)

Example sentences for saying *not* to do something.

- Favor de + **no** abrir + la boca.
  (*When "favor de" is used, place "no" before the action word.*)
- **No** es importante + levantarse.
  (*Use this structure with remaining beginnings.*)

Beginning	Action Word	Ending
Favor de Do me the favor of (i.e., Please)	**levantar(se)** to lift (yourself) (i.e., get up)	
Es necesario It is necessary	**abrir** to open	**la boca** the mouth
Es importante It is important	**mostrar(me)** to show (me)	**el brazo** the arm

Communicate about the Body

Table 1: The Head—La Cabeza

Choose the sentence beginning, add the action word, and add an ending if needed. Speak each sentence several times. For example:

Beginning	**Action Word**	**Ending**
Me gustaría *I would like*	examinarla. *to examine her.*	
Antes de *Before*	examinarle, *examining him,*	
favor de *do favor of*	ponerse *putting on*	el camisón. *the gown.*

Practice combining the Beginning column phrases with the Action Word phrases as they make sense. Add Ending column phrases if needed.

Beginning	Action Word	Ending
Favor de[10] Do me the favor of (i.e., Please)	**levantar(se)** to lift yourself/ himself/herself	**las amígdalas** the tonsils
Es necesario It is necessary	**abrir** to open	**la barbilla/ el mentón** the chin
Es importante It is important	**mostrar(me)** to show me	**la boca** the mouth
Es posible It is possible	**sentar(se)** to sit (yourself)	**el pelo** the hair, a hair
Es imposible It is impossible	**examinar(le)** to examine	**el cabello** the hair
Es fácil It is easy	**tomar la temperatura** to take the temperature	**el cuello** the neck
Es difícil It is difficult	**tocar** to touch	**los cachetes/ las mejillas** the cheeks
Me gustaría I would like	**mirar** to look at	**el cuero cabelludo** the scalp
Le gustaría He/she would like You would like		**las cejas** the eyebrows

Beginning	Action Word	Ending
Quiero I want **Quiere** He/she wants You want **Voy a** I am going to **Va a** He/she is going to You are going to **Vamos a** We are going to, Let's **Hay** (pron. "eye") There is, there are **Hay que** (pron. "eye") One needs **¿Hay que?** Does one need? **Tiene** She/he hasYou have **Tengo que** I have to **Tiene que** She/he has to You have to **Antes de** Before **Después de** After	**levantar(se)** to lift yourself/ himself/herself **abrir** to open **mostrar(me)** to show me **sentar(se)** to sit (yourself) **examinar(le)** to examine **tomar la temperatura** to take the temperature **tocar** to touch **mirar** to look at	**los dientes** the teeth **las encías** the gums **la frente** the forehead **la garganta** the throat **el globo ocular** the eyeball **las fosas nasales** the nostrils **la lengua** the tongue **los labios** the lips **la mandíbula** the jaw **la nariz** the nose **la nuez de Adán** Adam's apple **la nuca** the nape **el oído** the inner ear **el ojo** eye **los párpados** eyelids **las pestañas** eyelashes **la pupila** the pupil

Table 2: Upper Extremities—Extremidades Superiores

1. Combine each sentence beginning with action words and endings.
2. Speak each sentence several times.

Beginning	Action Word	Ending
Favor de Do me the favor of (i.e., Please) **Es necesario** It is ncccssary **Es importante** It is important **Es posible** It is possible **Es imposible** It is impossible **Es fácil** It is easy **Es dificil** It is difficult **Me gustaría** I would like **Le gustaría** He/she would like You would like	**levantar(se)** to lift yourself **abrir** to open **mostrar(me)** to show (me) **sentar(se)** to sit (yourself) **examinar(le)** to examine you **tomar la temperatura** to take the temperature	**la axila** the armpit **el antebrazo** the forearm **el brazo** the arm **el codo** the elbow **el dedo** the finger **el dedo anular** the ring finger **el dedo índice** the index finger **el dedo medio** the middle finger **el dedo meñique** the little finger

<table>
<tr>
<td>Quiero
I want

Quiere
He/she wants
You want

Voy a
I am going to

Va a
He/she is going to
You are going to

Vamos a
We are going to
Let’s

Hay que (pron. “eye”)
One needs
Does one need?

Tengo que
I have to

Tiene que
She/he has to
You have to

Antes de
Before

Después de
After</td>
<td>levantar(se)
to lift yourself

abrir
to open

mostrar(me)
to show (me)

sentar(se)
to sit (yourself)

examinar(le)
to examine you

tomar la temperatura
to take the temperature</td>
<td>el dedo pulgar
the thumb

el dorso de la mano
the back of the hand

la mano
the hand

la muñeca
the wrist

los nudillos
the knuckles

la palma de la mano
the palm

las uñas
the fingernails</td>
</tr>
</table>

Table 3: The Torso—El Tronco

1. Combine each sentence beginning with action words and endings.
2. Speak each sentence several times.

Beginning	Action Word	Ending
Favor de Do me the favor of (i.e., Please)	**levantar(se)** to lift (yourself/ himself/herself)	**los hombros** the shoulders
Es necesario It is necessary	**quitar(se)** to take off (yourself/ himself/herself)	**la clavícula** the collarbone
Es importante It is important	**mostrar(me)** to show (me)	**el pecho** the chest
Es posible It is possible	**sentar(se)** to sit (yourself/ himself/herself)	**el seno/los senos** the breast/breasts
Es imposible It is impossible	**examinar(le)** to examine	**la caja torácica** the rib cage
Me gustaría I would like	**poner(se)** to put on (yourself /himself/herself)	**las costillas** the ribs
Le gustaría He/she would like You would like		**la cintura** the waist
Quiero I want		**el abdomen** the abdomen
Quiere He/she wants You want		**el ombligo** the navel
Voy a I am going to		
Va a He/she is going to You are going to		

Beginning	Action Word	Ending
Vamos a We are going to Let's **Hay que** (pron. "eye") One needs Does one need? **Tengo que** I have to **Tiene que** She/he has to You have to **Antes de** Before **Después de** After	**levantar(se)** to lift (yourself/ himself/herself) **quitar(se)** to take off (yourself/ himself/herself) **mostrar(me)** to show (me) **sentar(se)** to sit (yourself/ himself/herself) **examinar(le)** to examine **poner(se)** to put on (yourself /himself/herself)	**los hombros** the shoulders **la clavícula** the collarbone **el pecho** the chest **el seno/los senos** the breast/breasts **la caja torácica** the rib cage **las costillas** the ribs **la cintura** the waist **el abdomen** the abdomen **el ombligo** the navel

Table 4: The Organs—Los Organos

1. Combine each sentence beginning with action words and endings.
2. Speak each sentence several times.

Beginning	Action Word	Ending
Favor de Do me the favor of (i.e., Please)	**levantar(se)** to lift (yourself/ himself/herself)	**las amígdalas** tonsils
Es necesario It is necessary	**quitar(se)** to take off (yourself/himself/ herself)	**el ano/el recto** rectum
Es importante It is important	**abrir** to open	**el cerebro** the brain
Es posible It is possible	**mostrar(me)** to show (me)	**la cerviz** the cervix
Es imposible It is impossible	**sentar(se)** to sit (yourself/ himself/herself)	**el colon** the colon
Es fácil It is easy	**examinar(le)** to examine	**el corazón** the heart
Es dificil It is difficult	**poner(se)** to put on (yourself /himself/ herself)	**el cuello uterino** the neck of the uterus, the cervix
Me gustaría I would like		**el bazo** **el espleen** the spleen
Le gustaría He/she would like You would like		**el estómago** stomach
Quiero I want		**el hígado** the liver
Quiere He/she wants You want		

Voy a I am going to **Va a** He/she is going to You are going to **Vamos a** We are going to Let's **Hay que** (pron. "eye") One needs Does one need? **Tengo que** I have to **Tiene que** She/he has to You have to **Antes de** Before **Después de** After		**el intestino** intestine **la matriz** womb **el miembro/ el pene** penis **el oído** inner ear **el ovario** the ovary **el pancreas** the pancreas **el riñón** the kidney **los testículos** the testicles **el útero** the uterus **la vágina** vagina **la vejiga** bladder **la vesícula biliar** gallbladder

Communicate about Common Medical Topics

Table 5: Women's Reproduction and Contraception

Use this table to communicate about women's contraception.

1. Combine each sentence beginning with action words and endings.
2. Speak each sentence several times.

Beginning	Action Word	Ending
Favor de Do me the favor of (i.e., Please)	**poner(se)** to put on (yourself)	**el método anticonceptivo** the method of contraception
Es necesario It is necessary	**explicar(le)** to explain (to you)	**el anillo** the ring
Es importante It is important	**saber** to know	**los aparatos intrauterinos** the intrauterine devices
Es posible It is possible	**dejar(le)** to allow or let (him/her/you)	**el condón** the condom
Es imposible It is impossible	**dejar de usar/tomar** stop using/taking	**el diafragma** the diaphragm
Es fácil It is easy	**sentar(se)** To sit (yourself/himself/herself)	**la ducha** the douche
Es dificil It is difficult	**examinar(le)** to examine (him/her/you/it)	**el escudo** the shield
Me gustaría I would like	**levantar(se)** to lift (yourself)	**el esperma** the sperm
Le gustaría He/she would like You would like	**empujar** to push	**el espiral** the spiral
Quiero I want	**controlar** to control	**las espumas** the foams
Quiere He/she wants You want	**subir a** to go up, get on	**la esterilización** sterilization
	bajar to go down	

Voy a I am going to **Va a** He/she is going to You are going to **Vamos a** We are going to Let's **Hay que** (pron. "eye") One needs Does one need? **Tengo que** I have to **Tiene que** She/he has to You have to **Antes de** Before **Después de** After	**tartar de mover** to try to move **mostrar(me)** To show me **mover** to move **acercar(se)** to move closer **usar** to use **comer** to eat **entender** to understand **poner(se)** To put on yourself/ himself/herself	**el gorro cervical** the cervical cap **el huevo** the egg **la jalea** the jelly **los lavados vaginales** douches **el lazo** the loop **el nudo** the bow **la ligadura de los tubos** tubal ligation **el método de ritmo** the rhythm method **la píldora** the pill **el profiláctico** the prophylactic **las relaciones sexuales** sexual relations **la retirada** withdrawal **la vasectomía** a vasectomy

Table 6: Pregnancies—Embarazos

In this table, we are going to use new sentence beginnings:

- **He tenido** I have had
- **¿Ha tenido?** Have you had? Has she had?
- **Uso** I use
- **Usa** She uses; you use
- **Dejo** I let/allow
- **Deja** She lets/allows; you let/allow

Beginning	Ending
Me gustaría I would like **¿Le gustaría?** Would she/you like? **Le gustaría** She/you would like **Quiero** I want **Quiere** You want She wants **Tengo** I have **¿Tiene?** Do you have? Does she have? **He tenido** I have had **Ha tenido?** Has she had? Have you had? **Uso** I use **Usa** She uses You use	**la regla, el período** menstrual period **la menstruación** menstrual period **estar embarazada** (also **estar encinta**, **estar preñada**, **estar en estado**) to be pregnant **múltiple embarazos** multiple pregnancies **otros embarazos** other pregnancies **el feto** the fetus **problemas de embarazo** problems of pregnancy • **rubeola** rubeola • **toxemia** toxemia • **presion alta** high blood pressure **dar a luz** give birth

Dejo de usar/tomar I quit using/taking **Deja de usar** She quits using/taking You quit using/taking **Antes de** Before **Después de** After	**parto** birth • **un parto prematuro** premature birth • **un parto por cesárea** a Cesarian section **la sala de partos** Delivery room **quedarse en el hospital** Stay in the hospital **la criatura** the infant • **el bebé** the baby boy • **la bebé** the baby girl • **el nené** the baby boy • **la nená** the baby girl **gemelos** twins **defectos de nacimiento** Birth defects **un aborto** an abortion • **accidental** miscarriage • **provocado** abortion • **terapéutico** therapeutic

Tables 7 and 8: Contagious Diseases—Enfermedades Contagiosos

Table 7: Definite Diagnosis

Beginning	Ending	
Usted tiene (Tiene) You have	**(la) cólera** cholera	**(la) poliomielitis** polio, poliomielitis
Tiene (Él tiene) He has	**(la) difteria** diphtheria	**(la) viruela** smallpox
Tiene (Ella tiene) She has	**(la) disentería** dysentery	**(las) viruelas locas** chicken pox
	(la) escarlatina scarlet fever	
Note: When giving a diagnosis, you often can omit the article (el, la, los, las).	**(la) fiebre amarilla** yellow fever	
	(el) hepatitis hepatitis	
	(la) malaria malaria	
	(la) meningitis meningitis	
	(el) paludismo malaria	
	(las) paperas mumps	
	(la) rubéola rubella, German measles	
	(el) sarampión measles	
	(el) tétano tetanus	
	(la) tifoidea typhoid	
	(la) tos ferina whooping cough	
	(la) tuberculosis tuberculosis	

Table 8: Possible Diagnosis

Use the beginning phrases in this table when the diagnosis is uncertain.

Beginning	Action Word	Ending
Es posible que It is possible that **Es imposible que** It is impossible that	**usted tenga** you may have **tenga (él tenga)** he may have **tenga (Ella tenga)** she may have	**(la) cólera** cholera **(la) difteria** diphtheria **(la) disentería** dysentery **(la) fiebre amarilla** yellow fever **(la) escarlatina** scarlet fever **(el) hepatitis** hepatitis **(la) malaria** malaria **(la) paludismo** malaria **(la) meningitis** meningitis **(las) paperas** mumps **(la) poliomielitis** polio, poliomielitis **(la) rubéola** rubella, German measles **(la) difteria** diphtheria **(la) disentería** dysentery **(la) fiebre amarilla** yellow fever **(el) sarampión** measles **(el) tétano** tetanus

Es posible que It is possible that **Es imposible que** It is impossible that	**usted tenga** You may have **tenga (él tenga)** he may have **tenga (ella tenga)** she may have	**(la) tuberculosis** tuberculosis **(la) tifoidea** typhoid **(la) viruela** smallpox **(las) viruelas locas** chicken pox **(el) hepatitis** hepatitis **(el) escarlatina** scarlet fever **(la) malaria** malaria **(la) paludismo** malaria **(la) meningitis** meningitis **(las) paperas** mumps **(la) poliomielitis** polio, poliomielitis **(la) rubéola** rubella, German measles **(el) sarampión** measles **(el) tétano** tetanus **(la) tos ferina** whooping cough **(la) tuberculosis** tuberculosis **(la) tifoidea** typhoid **(la) viruela** smallpox **(las) viruelas locas** chicken pox

Table 9: Medical Treatments—Los Tratamientos Médicos

1. Combine each sentence beginning with action words and endings.
2. Speak each sentence several times.

Beginning	Action Word	Ending
Hay que (pron. "eye") One needs Does one need? One must/ought to **Tengo que** I have to **Tiene que** She/he has to You have to	**dar** to give **inyectar** to inject **tener** to have	**una inmunización** an immunization **una inyección de antibiótico** an injection of antibiotic **una inyección de penicilina** an injection of penicillin **una inyección de refuerzo** an injection of booster **una inyección intravenosa** an intravenous injection **antibiótico** antibiotic **penicilina** penicillin **refuerzo** booster
Le va a picar. It is going to sting (you/him/her). **Va dar un picadura/piquete.** It is going to give a sting/little sting.		

Table 10: Explaining Procedures

Beginning	Action Word	Ending
Favor de Do me the favor of (i.e., Please)	**examinar** to examine	**el vientre** the womb
Es necesario It is necessary	**escuchar** to listen	**los pulmones** the lungs
Es importante It is important	**tomar** to take	**la temperatura** temperature
Es posible It is possible	**dar** to give	**un baño** A bath
Es imposible It is impossible	**poner** to put	**una receta** a prescription
Es fácil It is easy	**sacar** to take out	**una venda** a bandage
Es dificil It is difficult	**pesar** to weigh	**una sonda** a probe
Me gustaría I would like	**medir** to measure	**un suero** a serum
Le gustaría He/she would like You would like	**rasurar** to shave	**una sonda** a probe
Quiero I want	**voltear** to turn over	**un lavado** a wash
Quiere He/she wants You want	**cambiar** to change	**un yeso** a cast
Voy a I am going to	**ayudar** to help	**una radiografía** an X-ray
		un poquito de sangre a little blood

Va a He/she is going to You are going to **Vamos a** We are going to, Let's **Hay que** (pron. "eye") One needs Does one need? **Tengo que** I have to **Tiene que** She has to, He has to, You have to **Antes de** Before **Después de** After		

Table 11: Tests and Procedures—Exámenes y Procedimientos

Beginning	Action Word	Ending
Favor de Do me the favor of (i.e., Please)	**operar** to operate	**el alergia** (feminine word) allergy
Es necesario It is necessary	**preocuparse** to worry	**la anesthesia** the anesthesia
Es importante It is important	**durar** to last	**anestético** the anesthetic
Es posible It is possible	**apretar** to press/squeeze	**el asma** asthma
Es imposible It is impossible	**saber mal** to taste bad	**la cirugía** the surgery
Es fácil It is easy	**tratar de** to try to	**un catarro** a cold
Es dificil It is difficult	**funcionar mal** to malfunction	**la fiebre de heno** hay fever
Me gustaría I would like	**hacer una pregunta** to ask a question	**la sala de recuperación** the recovery room
Le gustaría He/she would like You would like	**hacer una radiografía** to take an X-ray	**la úlcera** the ulcer
Quiero I want	**insertar** to insert	**la máquina** the machine
Quiere He/she wants You want	**inyectar** to inject	**la prueba** the test
	molestar to bother	**el sistema digestivo** the digestive system

Voy a I am going to	**pararse** to stand	**el sulfato de bario** barium sulfate
Va a He/she is going to You are going to	**quedarse acostado/a** to remain lying down	**el tumor** the tumor
Vamos a We are going to Let's	**registrar la señal** to register/pick up the signal	**el catéter** catheter
Hay que (pron. "eye") One needs Does one need?	**sacar fotos** to take photos	**el conducto biliar** bile duct
Tengo que I have to	**penetrar** to penetrate	**las piedras biliares** gallstones
Tiene que She/he has to You have to	**correr el riesgo** to run the risk	**el riesgo** the risk
Antes de Before	**irritar** to irritate	**la tinta** the dye
Después de After	**sacar la orina** to remove urine	**el tubo** the tube
	proponerse to propose	**la vesícula biliar** the gallbladder
		anormalidades abnormalities
		las fotos the photos
		la materia radioactiva radioactive material
		el quiste the cyst
		una reacción alérgica an allergic reaction
		la sustancia radioactiva the radioactive substance
		el aparato

		the device/ the machine **el transmisor ultrasonido** ultrasound transmitter **incómodo** uncomfortable **la sonda catéter** the catheter probe **las piedras nefríticas** the kidney stones **la tinta** the dye **el yodo** iodine

Table 12: Physical Therapy—Terapia Física

1. Combine each sentence beginning with action words and endings.
   2. Speak each sentence several times.

Beginning	Action Word	Ending
Favor de Do me the favor of (i.e., Please)	**poner(se)** to put on (yourself)	**los ejercicios** the exercises
Es necesario It is necessary	**hacer** to do	**un puño** a fist
Es importante It is important	**dejar(le)** to allow or let (him/her/you)	**el dedo** the finger
Es posible It is possible	**sentar(se)** to sit (yourself)	**el bastón** the cane
Es imposible It is impossible	**levantar(se)** to lift (yourself)	**las aplicaciones calientes** hot compresses
Es fácil It is easy	**empujar** to push	**el aparato** the machine
Es dificil It is difficult	**enyesar** to put in a cast	**la máquina de ultrasonido** the ultrasound machine
Me gustaría I would like	**subir a** to go up, get on	**el masaje** the massage
Le gustaría He/she would like You would like	**bajar** to go down	**la silla de ruedas** the wheelchair
Quiero I want	**tratar de mover** to try to move	**el yeso** the cast
Quiere He/she wants You want	**mostrar(me)** To show (me)	**las muletas** the crutches
	mover to move	

Voy a I am going to **Va a** He/she is going to You are going to **Vamos a** We are going to Let's **Hay que** (pron. "eye") One needs Does one need? **Tengo que** I have to **Tiene que** She has to He has to You have to **Antes de** Before **Después de** After	**acercar(se)** to move closer **usar** to use **comer** to eat	**en cabestrillo** in a sling **el torniquete** the tourniquet **los tratamientos** the treatments **la mano** the hand **el dedo anular** the ring finger **el dedo índice** the index finger **el dedo medio** the middle finger **el dedo meñique** the little finger **el dedo pulgar** the thumb

Communicate about Emergencies

You might need to deal with patients who experience an emergency at the beach, in a restaurant, or in a fire.

Beach—Words to Learn

English	Spanish
waves on the towel lifeguard tower	olas en la toalla torre de salvavidas
sand on top of the sand close to the sand castle	arena encima de la arena cerca del castillo de arena
close to children seagulls crying	cerca de los niños gritan (shouting)

Restaurant—Words to Learn

English	Spanish
coughing a fainting spell, blackout	tosiendo un desmayo

Fire—Words to Learn

English	Spanish
suffocation fire a fire	asfixia fuego un incendio

Table 13: Emergencies

1. Combine each sentence beginning with the possible endings.
2. Speak each sentence several times.

Beginning	Ending
¿Dónde está ... Where is ...? **¿Dónde están ...** Where are ...?	**el paciente** **la victima** **el niño** **el juvenil** **la niña** **el accidente**
Tiene She/he has You have **Hay** There is, there are **Pierde** She/he is losing You are losing **Es** She/he is You are	**un accidente** an accident **un ahogo** a drowning **una puñalada** a stabbing **un atento a suicidio** a suicide attempt **un desmayo** a fainting **una sobredosis/** **una dosis** an overdose **una dosis excesiva** an overdose **las drogas** drugs **un enveneno** a poisoning

¿Está?
Is she/he
Are you

Pierde
She/he is losing
You are losing

Hay (pron. "eye")
There is/are

Hay que (pron. "eye")
One needs
Does one need?

Tengo que
I have to

- **poner**
  to put
- **enyesar**
  to cast/put in a cast
- **dar**
  to give

Tiene que
She/he has to
You have to

- **poner**
  to put
- **enyesar**
  to cast/put in a cast
- **dar**
  to give

Tengo
I have

Tiene
She/he has
You have

Consciente
Conscious

Conocimiento
Consciousness

una fractura
a fracture

una hemorragia
a hemorrhage

una quemadura
a burn

sangre
blood

el yeso
the cast

el cuchillo
the knife

la pistola/el revólver
pistol/revolver

la ambulancia
the ambulance

la camilla
the stretcher

el camillero
stretcher-bearer

el oxígeno
the oxygen

la respiración artificial
artificial respiration

Está Sagrando*
She/he is bleeding
You are bleeding

Communicate about Daily Habits

Table 15: Daily Habits Relating to Others

Spanish speakers talk about daily habits differently from the way English speakers do.

- The Spanish speaker says, in English translation, "**He** washes **himself** the hair."
- An English speaker says, "**He** washes **his** hair."

- The Spanish speaker says, "**Se** llama …"
- An English speaker says, "**He** calls **himself** …" or "**She** calls **herself** …" or "**You** call **yourself** ..."

Use the following chart to talk about daily habits. As you use these patterns, they will come naturally.

Examples for Using This Table

Mario, es necesario ducharse.
Mario, it is necessary to shower yourself.

Va a bañarse.
He is going to bathe himself.

¿Antes de tomar pastillas hay que desayunarse?
Before taking pills does one need to eat breakfast?

Beginning	Action Word
Favor de Do me the favor of **Es necesario** It is necessary **Es importante** It is important **Es posible** It is possible	**cepillarse** to brush himself/herself/yourself **peinarse el pelo** to comb himself/herself/yourself the hair **ducharse** to shower himself/herself/yourself **rasurarse** to razor (shave) himself/herself/yourself

Es imposible
It is impossible

Es fácil
It is easy

Es dificil
It is difficult

Le gustaría
He/she would like
You would like

Quiere
He/she wants
You want

Va a
He/she is going to
You are going to

Hay que (pron. “eye”)
One needs
Does one need?

Tiene que
He/she has to
You have to

Antes de
Before

Después de
After

despertarse
to awaken himself/herself/yourself

sentarse
to sit himself/herself/yourself

bañarse
to bathe himself/herself/yourself

secarse
to dry himself/herself/yourself the body

secarse el pelo
to dry himself/herself/yourself the hair

ponerse
to put on himself/herself/yourself

desayunarse
to breakfast himself/herself/yourself

dormirse
to fall sleep

lavarse
to wash himself/herself/yourself

irse
to leave (he, she, you leave)

Table 16: Daily Habits Relating to Self

Spanish speakers talk about daily habits differently from the way English speakers do.

- The Spanish speaker says, "I wash **myself** the hair."
- An English speaker says, "**I** wash **my** hair."

- The Spanish speaker says, "Me llamo …"
- An English speaker says, "I call myself …"

Use the table below to talk in the first person about daily habits. As you use these patterns, they will come (and you will understand them) naturally.

Examples for Using the Following Table

Es necesario *ducharme.*
It is necessary to shower myself.

Tengo que *sentarme.*
I have to sit down.

Voy a *bañarme.*
I am going to bathe myself.

¿Antes de tomar pildoras, *es necesario desayunarme?*
Before taking pills, does one need to eat breakfast?

Beginning	Action Word
Favor de Do me the favor of	**cepillarme** to brush myself
Es necesario It is necessary	**peinarme el pelo** to comb myself the hair
Es importante It is important	**ducharme** to shower myself
Es posible It is possible	**rasurarme** to razor (shave) myself
Es imposible It is impossible	**despertarme** to awaken myself
Es fácil It is easy	**sentarme** to sit myself
Es dificil It is difficult	**bañarme** to bathe myself
Me gustaría I would like	**secarme** to dry myself
Quiero I want	**secarme el pelo** to dry myself the hair
Voy a I am going to	**ponerme** to put on myself
Hay que (pron. "eye") One needs Does one need?	**desayunarme** to breakfast myself
Tengo que I have to	**dormirme** to fall asleep (I sleep)
Antes de Before	**lavarme** to wash myself
Después de After	**irme** to leave (I leave)

Chapter 5: Practicing with the CD

Introduction

The companion CD, *Spanish for Fun and Forever*, is an important component of this self-study book. If you have the CD, listen to Track 1 while you read the following transcript. You will be introduced to the methods used in the CD tracks. These methods help you learn Spanish quickly and easily. You will also learn what content each CD track teaches.

How to Obtain This CD

You can obtain *Spanish for Fun and Forever* from www.caminoespanol.com, www.amazon.com, www.cdbaby.com, or www.itunes.com.

Transcripts in This Chapter

Transcript of Track 1: Introduction

Welcome to *Speak Spanish Now*. This series is called *Spanish for Fun and Forever*. My name is Murney Blades.

In this series you will have the opportunity to hear:

- A medical component
  - with yes/no answers; and
  - short answers.
- Mix-and-match Spanish system
- Speech patterns unique to Spanish
- Vocabulary for use
  - at the beach;
  - in the restaurant;
  - at the dance;
  - in the park; and
  - daily habits, etc.

The English speaker repeats twice for clarification. The student cannot repeat what he cannot hear or distinguish.

For example, the student listener hears, "Y a veces escucho."
Did he hear …

- *Ya ves*, which means, "Now [or already] you see"?
- *Llaves*, which means, "keys"?
- *Y a veces*, which means, "and at times"?

He heard, "Y a veces escucho," which translates to, "And at times I listen [or I hear]."

Regarding translation, we strive for communication of the *message*.

- What English speakers call a "good translation" is general.
- And what English speakers call a "poor translation" is precise.

Example: The Spanish speaker says,

- **"Pienso ir al cine."**
  I *think* to go to the movies. (*Precise*)
  This exact translation may confuse the listener.

- **"Pienso ir al cine."**
  I *plan* to go to the movies. (*General*)
  The message is clear. The listener understands.

We are striving for communication using the general meaning of word groups.

- **Tengo hambre** = "I have hunger" or "I am hungry."
- **Tengo sed** = "I have thirst" or "I am thirsty."
- **Tengo miedo** = "I have fear" or "I am afraid."
- **Tengo cinco años** = "I have five years" or "I am five years old."

Among the mix-and-match **sentence starters** you hear throughout are:

- **Voy a** = I am going to
- **Va a** = She or he is going to, or usted (you formal) are going to
- **Vamos a** = We are going to
- **Tengo que** = I have to
- **Tiene que** = You have to
- **Puede** = You can or are able
- **Favor de** = Do me the favor of, or please

You will hear special patterns in the first person (I) and the third person (he, she, usted = formal you). It is far easier to learn the special patterns and substitute vocabulary as needed.

Example:
Me duele la cabeza.   **Cabeza** is head.
Me duele la cabeza.   The head hurts me, or I have a headache.

Substitute **estómago** (estómago = stomach).
Me duele el estomago = the stomach hurts me, or I have a stomachache.
Le duele would indicate "it hurts him/her/usted."
Once we've learned the "Me duele"/"Le duele" pattern, we can incorporate similar patterns:

- **Me gusta**, which means "I like" (**Me gusta la comida méxicana** = I like Mexican food).
- **Me falta**, which means "I'm missing" (**Me falta la servilleta** = I'm missing the napkin).

This CD is an introduction to *Speaking Spanish Now*. As in English, there are many nuances. The goal of this series is immediate, simple communication. Remember:
Spanish is specific, precise. English is more general.
Our goal is the *communication, the message*.

Introduction to Tracks on CD

As you listen to these recordings, you will want to focus on certain vocabulary and sentence structures to meet your immediate needs.

Track 2 models how to introduce yourself and ask for a person's name.

Track 3 gives an introduction to numbers and their uses.

Track 4 teaches the numbers.

If you are a health professional, a firefighter, or a paramedic, you may wish to first focus on **Tracks 5, 6,** and **7**, entitled "First Responder Questions," "Emergency Room (the Hospital)," and "The Paramedics."

You will hear

- types of injuries;
- how to ask if it hurts;
- level of pain;
- descriptions of the pain; and
- current medications—prescribed or natural.

You will note that the first person (I) and the third person (she, he, usted) are always used.

Some tracks are fun and yet include vocabulary necessary if an accident were to occur at the beach or in a restaurant.

Track 8 includes beach vocabulary.
Track 9 gives a restaurant scene.

One of my personal favorites is "The Dance" on **Track 10**, which includes

- body parts; and
- expressions such as *up*, *down*, etc.

In "Relaxation," **Track 11**, you will hear

- additional body parts;
- a relaxation exercise for calming yourself or others; and
- a visualization.

"Daily Routine [Habits]," **Track 12**, uses special expressions unique to Spanish. Here, expressions such as fear and hunger are used.

"Fire," **Track 13**, focuses on evacuation vocabulary in the event of a sudden emergency.

"Emotions" on **Track 14** deals with personal injury and the emotions involved. Here, you hear the words for bruises and how to express fear used in context.

In closing, **there is no correct way to listen to these recordings**. Listen to what you need now.

- The key is to have fun!
- Dance with the dance!
- Relax with the relaxation!

Remember, have fun.

Transcript of Track 2: What Is Your Name?

¿Cómo se llama? Can mean:

- What's your name?
- What's his name?
- What's her name?

¿Cómo se llama? (What's your name?) **¿Cómo se llama?**

- **Me llamo Marita Rosales**. (My name is Marita Rosales.)

Mucho gusto. (Much pleasure.)
El gusto es mío. (The pleasure's mine.)

Yo me llamo Marita Rosales. (My name is Marita Rosales.)

¿Cómo se llama?

- **Yo me llamo Marita.**
- **Él se llama Juan.**
- **Ella se llama Juana.**

¿Cómo se llama él? (What's his name?) **¿Cómo se llama él?**

- **Él se llama Juan Ramón.** (His name is Juan Ramón.)
- **Él se llama Juan Ramón.** (His name is Juan Ramón.)

¿Cómo se llama ella? (What's her name?) **¿Cómo se llama ella?**

- **Ella se llama Juana Méndez.** (Her name is Juana Méndez.)
- **Ella se llama Juana Méndez.** (Her name is Juana Méndez.)

¿Cómo se llama?

- **Yo me llamo Marita.**
- **Él se llama Juan.**
- **Ella se llama Juana.**

¿Cómo se llama usted? ¿Cómo se llama usted?

- **Me llamo Murney Blades.** (My name is Murney Blades.)

Mucho gusto. (Much pleasure.)
El gusto es mío. (The pleasure is mine.)

Yo me llamo Murney Blades. (My name is Murney Blades.)
Es un placer. (It's a pleasure.)
Nos vemos. (We'll see each other.)

¡En la playa! (On the beach!)
En un restaurante? (In a restaurant?)
¡Buena idea! (Good idea!)

Transcript of Track 3: Introduction to Numbers

We use numbers in many ways.
We express:

Age:

- **Tengo vientun años.** (I have twenty-one years. I am twenty-one years old.) **Tengo vientiun años.**

Level of pain:

- **Siete.** (Seven.) **Siete.**

Weight:

- **Ciento vienticinco libras.** (One hundred twenty-five pounds.) **Ciento veinticinco libras.**

Height:

- **Cinco pies.** (Five feet.) **Cinco pies.**
- **Cinco pies, cuatro pulgadas.** (Five feet, four inches.) **Cinco pies, cuatro pulgadas.**

Pulse:

- **Sesenta y siete.** (Sixty-seven.) **Sesenta y siete.**

Temperature:

- **Noventa y nueve grados.** (Ninety-nine degrees.) **Noventa y nueve grados.**

Blood pressure:

- **Ciento veinte sobre ochenta. Ciento veinte sobre ochenta.** (One hundred twenty over eighty.) **Ciento veinte sobre ochenta.**

Time:

- **Es la una.** (It is one o'clock.)
- **Son las dos.** (It is two.)
- **Son las tres.** (It is three.)

Prices in stores and restaurants:

- **¿Cuánto cuesta?** (How much does it cost?)
- **Cinco dólares.** (Five dollars.) **Cinco dólares.**

Transcript of Track 4: Numbers

Numbers:

One—**Uno**	Five—**Cinco**
Two—**Dos**	Six—**Seis**
Three—**Tres**	Seven—**Siete**
Four—**Cuatro**	Eight—**Ocho**

How many years have (are) you? **¿Cuántos años tiene usted?**

Nine—**Nueve**	Thirteen—**Trece**
Ten—**Diez**	Fourteen—**Catorce**
Eleven—**Once**	Fifteen—**Quince**
Twelve—**Doce**	

Yo tengo quince años. I have (am) fifteen years.

¿Cuántos años tiene? How old are you?

¿Cuántos años tiene?
Yo tengo quince años.

Now we add:

- Ten and six. **Diez y seis (dieciséis).**
- Twenty and one. **Veinte y uno (veintíuno).**
- Thirty and three. **Treinta y tres.**
- Forty-four. **Cuarenta y cuatro.**
- Fifty-five. **Cincuenta y cinco.**

¿Cuántos años tiene <u>él</u>? How many years does he have?

- Sixty-six. **Sesenta y seis.**
- Seventy-seven. **Setenta y siete.**
- Eighty-eight. **Ochenta y ocho.**
- Ninety-nine. **Noventa y nueve.**

Él tiene treinta años. He has thirty years.

- One hundred—**Cien**
- One hundred one—**Ciento uno**
- One hundred ten—**Ciento diez**
- One hundred twenty—**Ciento veinte**

How many years has <u>she</u>? **¿Cuántos años tiene <u>ella</u>?**

- One hundred thirty—**Ciento treinta**
- One hundred forty—**Ciento cuarenta**
- One hundred fifty—**Ciento cincuenta**
- One hundred sixty—**Ciento sesenta**

¿Cuántos años tiene ella? How old is she?
Ella tiene noventa años. She has ninety years.

¿Cuántos años tiene él? How old is he?
Él tiene noventa años. He has ninety years.

¿Cuántos años tiene ella? How old is she?
Ella tiene cien años. She has one hundred years.

Estos son los numeros. These are the numbers.

[The focus of this recording is to emphasize the pronunciation *and* how to ask and answer questions pertaining to age. Please note that *¿Cuántos años tiene?* can be used to inquire about his age, her age, or your age (respectful/formal you). In the tens and all decades, use "y" to signify "and." Thus, to say sixteen, one says "ten and six," *diez y seis*; to say thirty-three, one says "thirty and three," *treinta y tres*. A more detailed explanation of numbers and time can be found on the following websites: http://www.studyspanish.com/lessons/cardnum3.htm (counting); http://www.studyspanish.com/lessons/time.htm (telling time).]

Transcript of Track 5: First Responder Questions in Emergency

Important: If you are a first responder, also study tracks 6, 7, and 13.

[Following are] first responder questions in an emergency, structured for yes/no (sí/no) and one-word answers.

Tranquilos, por favor.	Calm, please.
Alenjense, por favor.	Move back, please
Atrás, por favor.	Back, please.
¿Se cortó?	Did you cut yourself?
¿Se quemó?	Did you burn yourself?
¿Se torció?	Did you twist yourself?
¿Se fracturó?	Did you fracture yourself?
¿Se raspó?	Did you scrape yourself?
¿Hueso roto?	Broken bone?
¿Moretón?	Bruise?
¿Cómo se siente usted?	How do you feel?
¿Se siente bien?	Do you feel well?
¿Se siente mal?	Do you feel bad?
¿Se siente bien?	
¿Se siente mal?	
¿Bien? ¿O mal?	
¿Bien? ¿O mal?	
¿Cómo se siente?	
¿Cómo se siente?	
¿Cómo se siente usted?	How do you feel?
• **Me siento mal.**	I feel bad.
¿Cómo se siente <u>él</u>?	How does <u>he</u> feel?
• **Se siente bien.**	He feels well.
¿Cómo se siente <u>ella</u>?	How does <u>she</u> feel?
• **Se siente mal.**	She feels bad.
¿Cómo se siente usted?	
¿Cómo se siente él?	
¿Cómo se siente ella?	

¿Cómo es el dolor? How is the pain?

- **Número uno, menor.** Number one, minor.
- **Número diez, el peor.** Number ten, the worst.

¿Cómo es el dolor? How is the pain?

- **Número uno, menor; número diez, el peor.**
- **Número uno, menor; número diez, el peor.**

¿Cómo se siente? ¿Cómo es el dolor? How is the pain?

- **¿Sordo?** Dull?
- **¿Agudo?** Sharp?
- **¿O constante?** Or constant?
- **¿Palpitante?** Palpitating?

¿Cómo es el dolor? ¿Cómo es el dolor?

- **¿Sordo, agudo o constante, palpitante?**
- **¿Sordo, agudo o constante, palpitante?**

¿Cómo es el dolor? How is the pain?

- **¿Va y viene?** Does it go and come?
- **¿O se quita?** Or does it quit?

¿Va y viene? ¿Va y viene?
¿O se quita? ¿O se quita?

¿Cómo se siente? ¿Cómo es el dolor?

- **Número uno, menor. Número diez, el peor.**

¿Sordo, agudo o constante?
¿Palpitante?
¿Va y viene?
¿O se quita?
¿Cómo es el dolor?
¿Cómo es el dolor?

Transcript of Track 6: Emergency Room

Important: If you are a first responder, also study tracks 5, 7, and 13.

The ambulance arrives. Someone is on a stretcher. The person has an injury.

- **La camilla.** Stretcher.
- **Tiene una herida.** He has an injury.
- **Una quemadura.** A burn.

Speaker	Spoken Words
Nurse	**¿Qué pasó?** What happened? **¿Qué pasó?**
Patient	**Me quemé.**
Nurse	**¿Me quemé?** Oh! You burned yourself. **Se quemó. Se quemó.**
Nurse	**¿Cómo? ¿Con ácido? ¿Cómo?** **¿Quemadura?** **¿Una quemadura eléctrica?** An electric burn? **¿O con ácido**? With acid? **¿Con ácido?**
Patient	**Con el agua hirviendo.**
Nurse	Water? Boiling water? **¿Agua hirviendo?** **Agua hirviendo.**
Patient	**Me duele. Me duele.**
Nurse	**Le duele.** I know it hurts. **Le duele.** It hurts you. **Le duele.**
Patient	**Me duele el brazo. Me duelen las manos.**
Nurse	**Le duelen las manos.** Your hands hurt. **Le duelen las manos.**
Nurse	**Es una quemadura seria.** A serious burn. **Es una quemadura seria.** **Tiene que ingresar al hospital.** **Tiene que** You have to **ingresar** admit yourself **al hospital.** to the hospital.

	Tiene que ingresar al hospital.
Patient	**¿Voy a ingresar?**
Nurse	**Si. Va a ingresar.** Yes! You are going to be admitted. **Ingresar. Va a ingresar al hospital.**

Someone has a cut on the head.

Speaker	**Spoken Words**
Patient	**Me caí.**
Nurse	**Me caí.** I fell. You fell? **¿Se cayó? ¿Se cayó?**
Patient	**Me corté en una piedra.**
Nurse	**Me corté.** I cut myself. Oh! You cut yourself! **Se cortó. Se cortó.** You have a bad cut.
Patient	**¿Tiene que dar puntos?**
Nurse	**Tengo que dar puntos.** I have to put in stitches. **Tengo que dar puntos. Dar puntos.**
Patient	**Tengo miedo.**
Nurse	**Tiene miedo.** You're afraid. You have fear. **Tiene miedo.**
Patient	**Necesito agua. Tengo sed.**
Nurse	You need water? **Agua. Tiene sed?** You have thirst? You're thirsty? **Tiene sed.**
Nurse	**Tengo que limpiar, desinfectar y vendar la herida.** **Limpiar.** To clean. **Limpiar.** **Desinfectar.** To disinfect. **Desinfectar.** **Vendar.** To bandage. **La herida.** **Tengo que limpiar, desinfectar y vendar la herida.** The injury. **Vendar la herida.**
Patient	**¿Puedo regresar a mi casa?**
Nurse	**Si, puede.** You can. **Regresar.** Return. **A casa.** Home. **Sí, puede regresar a casa.**
Patient	**Okay. Gracias.**

A child has eaten poison.

Speaker	Spoken Words
Mother	**Mi hija se envenenó. Se envenenó.**
Nurse	Your daughter? **¿Hija?** Poisoned herself? **¿Su hija se envenenó?** **¿Tu hija se envenenó? ¿Se envenenó?** **¿Tomó veneno?** Ate poison? Wow! **¿Qué tomó?** What did she take? **¿Qué tomó?**
Mother	**Este es el frasco.**
Nurse	**El frasco.** The bottle. **El frasco.** **¿Vomitó?** Did she vomit? **¿Vomitó?**
Mother	**Un poco.**
Nurse	**Vamos a hacer un lavado.** We're going to do a wash. **Un lavado del estómago.** **Hacer un lavado del estómago.**
Mother	**¿Espero aquí?**
Nurse	**Sí. Espere.** Yes. Wait. **Espere.**

In this situation we hear:

Marita **Le duele el brazo.**

Murney **Le duele el brazo.** The arm hurts.

Marita **Le duelen las manos.**

Murney **Le duelen las manos.** The hands hurt.

We also learn special expressions:

Marita **Tengo miedo.**

Murney **Tengo miedo.** I have fear, or I'm afraid.

Marita **Tengo sed.**

Murney **Tengo sed.** I have thirst, or I'm thirsty.

Transcript of Track 7: Paramedics

Important: If you are a first responder, also study tracks 5, 6, and 13.

The paramedics received an emergency call. We're at the house now.

Speaker	Spoken Words
Paramedic	**¿Qué pasó?** What happened? **¿Qué pasó?**
Patient	**Me caí.**
Paramedic	Fell? **¿Se cayó?** You fell? **Se cayó.**
Patient	**Sí, me caí.**
Paramedic	**¿Cómo se siente?** How do you feel? **¿Cómo se siente? ¿Se siente bien?** Well? **¿O se siente mal?** Badly? **¿Bien o mal?**
Patient	**No muy bien.**
Paramedic	**No muy bien.** Not very well? **¿No muy bien?**
Patient	**No.**
Paramedic	**¿Cómo es el dolor?** How is the pain? **Número uno, menor**. Number one, the least. **Número diez, el peor.** The worst. **Número uno, menor**. **Número diez, peor.**
Patient	**Siete.**
Paramedic	Seven? **Siete. Siete.**
Paramedic	**Cómo es el dolor?** How is the pain? • **¿Sordo?** Dull? • **¿Agudo?** Sharp? • **¿Constante?** Constant? • **¿Palpitante?** Palpitating, throbbing? **¿Sordo? ¿Agudo? ¿Constante? ¿Palpitante? ¿Cómo es el dolor?** • **¿Va y viene?** Goes and comes. • **¿O se quita?** It quits.
Patient	**Se quita y regresa**.

Paramedic	**Se quita**. It stops. **Y Regresa?** And it returns. **Regresa.**
Patient	**Creo que me fracturé el tobillo.**
Paramedic	**¿El tobillo?** Ankle. **Tobillo.** **¿Se fracturó? Se fracturó.**
Paramedic	**Voy a llevarla al hospital**. I am going to take you to the hospital. **Vamos a llevarla al hospital**. We're going to take you to the hospital. **En ambulancia.** In an ambulance. **En ambulancia.**

In the emergency room. **La sala de emergencia. La sala de emergencia.**

Nurse	What's your name? **¿Cómo se llama?**
Patient	**Angélica Chacón.**
Nurse	**Angélica Chacón.** **¿Alguna enfermedad?** An illness? **¿Enfermedad?**
Patient	**Diabetis.**
Nurse	**Diabetis. Diabetis**. Diabetes in English. **¿Toma medicina?** Do you take medicine? **¿Toma medicina?**
Patient	**Sí.**
Nurse	**¿Receta médica?** Prescription? **¿Receta médica?**
Patient	**Sí, receta médica.**
Nurse	**¿Otra?** Another? **¿Naturál?** Natural? **¿Hierbas?** Herbs? **¿Hierbas?**
Patient	**Nada más.**
Nurse	**Nada más?** Nothing more? **¿Alergias a medicina? ¿Alergias?**
Patient	**Sí, penicilina.**

Nurse	**¿Penicilina? ¿Penicilina?** Penicillin in English.
Nurse	**¿Cuándo comió?** When did you eat?
Patient	**Hace tres horas.**
Nurse	Three hours ago? **Hace tres horas. Hace tres horas.**
	¿Cuándo tomó? When did you drink? **¿Cuándo tomó?**
Patient	**Hace dos horas.**
Nurse	**Hace dos horas**. Two hours ago? **¿Hace dos horas?**
Nurse	**La presión de sangre.** The blood pressure. **La presión de sangre es ciento veinte** (120) **sobre ochenta** (80), **one twenty** (120) **over eighty** (80).
Nurse	**El pulso.** The pulse. **El pulso es setenta y dos.** Seventy-two (72).
Nurse	**La temperatura es noventa y nueve grados.** The temperature is ninety-nine (99) degrees.
Patient	**¿La temperatura es noventa y nueve grados?**
Nurse	**Sí.**
	Espere en la camilla, por favor. Wait on the stretcher, please. **Espere en la camilla, por favor**.
Patient	**¿Es necesario tomar rayos-X?**
Nurse	**Sí, es necesario tomar rayos-X.** It is necessary to take X-rays. **Sí, es necesario tomar rayos-X.**

What you just heard are two situations you might encounter on a routine day.

Transcript of Track 8: The Beach

A child says, "Look at the seagulls."

Speaker	Spoken Words
Murney	**¿Marita, cómo se dice "seagull"?**
Marita	**Se dice "gaviota."**
Murney	**¿Gaviota?** Seagull. **Gaviota.** Seagull.
Murney	Listen to the waves.
Marita	**¿Las olas?**
Murney	**Las olas.**
Marita	**Sí, olas.**
Murney	**Olas.** Waves.
Murney	Feel the sand.
Marita	**¡Oh! ¿Arena?**
Murney	**"La arena"** is sand?
Marita	**Sí. Mira el castillo.**
Murney	**¿Castillo?** Castle?
Marita	**El castillo de arena.**
Murney	Oh! Sand castle. **El castillo de arena. Castillo de arena.**
Murney	I feel the breeze.
Marita	**¡La brisa!**
Murney	**"La brisa"** is breeze?
Marita	**Sí. La brisa.**
Marita	**Mira la concha.**
Murney	Seashell?
Marita	**Sí, las conchas.**

Murney	**Las conchas.** Seashells.
	[Sound of children laughing]
Marita	**Las gaviotas gritan.**
Murney	**¿Gritan? ¡Gritan!** They're screaming. [Sound of seagulls crying]
	[Sound of children laughing]
Marita	**¿Los niños se rien?**
Murney	**¿Niños?** Children, right?
Marita	**Sí! Se rien.**
Murney	**¿Se rien?** They are laughing.
Marita	**Sí, los niños se rien.**
Murney	**Niños.** Children. **Se rien.** They are laughing.
Marita	**El niño sobre la toalla usa los lentes de sol.**
Murney	**¿La toalla?** Towel?
Marita	**La toalla.**
Murney	**La toalla.** Towel. **"Sol"** is sun! **¿Lentes de sol?** Sunglasses?
Marita	**Sí, sí.**
Murney	**Los lentes de sol.** Sunglasses.

Speaker	**Spoken Words**
Murney	**¿Cómo se dice "lifeguard tower"?**
Marita	**La torre de salvavidas.**
Murney	Is tower **"torre"?**
Marita	**Sí, torre del salvavidas.**
Murney	**El salvavidas.** Lifeguard. **¡Salvavidas!**

	Children in the ocean!
Marita	**Los niños van a nadar en el mar.**
Murney	**Niños.** Children. **Mar.** Ocean.
Marita	**Van a nadar.**
Murney	Does **"nadar"** mean "to swim"?
Marita	**Sí, van a nadar.**
Murney	They're going to swim.
Marita	**Murney, hace calor.**
Murney	It is hot! Let's go!

Transcript of Track 9: The Restaurant

Marita and I have left the beach, and we're now approaching a restaurant.

Speaker	Spoken Words
Marita	**Murney, tengo hambre**.
Murney	**¿Hambre?** You have hunger? You're hungry? **¿Tiene hambre? ¿Tiene hambre?**
Marita	**¿Vamos a un restaurante?**
Murney	Yes! Let's go to a restaurant! **Vamos a un restaurante.** **Vamos.** Let's go! **A un restaurante.** **¿Adónde?** Where? **¿Adónde?**
Marita	**A mi restaurante favorito. El vegetariano.**
Murney	**¿Restaurante favorito?** Favorite restaurant? Oh! **Restaurante favorito.** **¿Es vegetariano?** It's vegetarian? **Vegetariano. Vegetariano.**
Marita	**Mesa para dos, por favor. Lejos de la música.**
Murney	**Mesa para dos.** Table for two. **Mesa para dos.** **¿Lejos de la música? ¿Lejos?** Far? Far from the music. **Lejos.**
Marita	**Para conversar y escuchar la música.**
Murney	To talk and listen to the music. **Para conversar y escuchar.** **Conversar y escuchar.**

At the table, they hear ...

Marita	**¡Escuche! Una persona tiene tos.**
Murney	A person has a cough? **¿Eh, una persona tiene tos? Tiene tos.**
Marita	**El mesero le da agua.**
Murney	Yes, the waiter gives him water. **Mesero.** Waiter. **Da agua.** Gives water. **Agua.**
Marita	**La carta, por favor.**
Murney	The menu, please. **"Carta"** is menu?
Murney	**Marita! ¿Dónde está el baño?** Where's the bathroom? **¿Dónde está el baño?**
Marita	**Derecho y a la izquierda**.
Murney	**Derecho.** Straight. **Derecho.** **Y.** And to the left? **¿Izquierda?** Left. **Izquierda.** I can't wait to tell you about my trip to Texas when I get back.
Murney	**¿Qué le gusta comer?**
Marita	**Mi plato favorito es un taco orgánico.**
Murney	**¿Un taco orgánico?** An organic taco? **¿Su favorito?** Your favorite? **¿Su favorito?**
Marita	**¡Me falta la servilleta!**
Murney	**Me falta la servilleta.** Missing. Missing the napkin! I'm missing the napkin. **La servilleta. La servilleta.**
Marita	**La comida está deliciosa.**
Murney	Yes, the food is delicious. **La comida está deliciosa. ¡La comida está deliciosa!**

Marita	**¡Escuche a los hombres guapos!**
Murney	**Guapos.** Handsome. **¡Guapos!** **Escuche a los hombres.** Listen to the men. **Escuche a los hombres.** **Guapos.** Handsome. **¡Guapos!**
Murney	**¿Dónde?**
Marita	**A la derecha.** **Camarera, por favor. La cuenta.**
Murney	Waitress, please. **Camarera.** Waitress. **Camarera, la cuenta.** The check. **La cuenta.**
Marita	**Oh! La propina.**
Murney	The tip. **La propina.** [Sounds of people talking] **Vamos.** Let's go.

Transcript of Track 10: The Dance

In this presentation, you will hear body parts and movements, such as open, close, turn, etc.

[Note that *derecho* (right), used in this track, is an adjective and must agree with the noun it describes. Example: *el brazo derecho* = the right arm; *la pierna derecha* = the right leg. However, in giving and asking directions, one often hears *derecho*. Here the word means "straight" on. The colloquial "right on" captures the meaning.]

Speaker	Spoken Words
Marita	**¡Murney, a bailar!**
Murney	Marita! Show me how to dance! I love that music and the way you dance. **¡Enseñeme!** Teach me. **¡Enseñeme!**
Marita	**Yo siento la música.**
Murney	**Yo siento.** I feel. Oh! You feel the music. **Siente.** **Usted siente la música. Usted siente la música.**
Marita	**Sigo el ritmo.**
Murney	**¿Sigo?** I follow. **Sigo el ritmo.** Rhythm. You follow the rhythm. **Usted sigue el ritmo. Sigue el ritmo.**
Marita	**Voy a mover el cuerpo.**
Murney	You are going to move the body. **Mover el cuerpo.** Move the body. **Va a mover el cuerpo.**
Marita	**Brazo derecho adelante.**
Murney	**"Brazo"** is arm. **¿Sí?** Yes! Right arm! **Brazo derecho. Brazo derecho.** **¡Adelante**! Forward. **¡Adelante!**
Marita	**Brazo izquierdo adelante.**
Murney	Left arm. **Brazo izquierdo, adelante**. Forward. **Adelante.**

Marita **Las manos hacia arriba.**

Murney **Las manos.** Hands. **Las manos.** **Arriba.** Up. **Arriba.**

Marita **Las manos hacia abajo.**

Murney **"Abajo"** is down. **Abajo. Las manos hacia abajo.**

Marita **A mover las caderas.**

Murney Let's move the hips. **Caderas.** Hips. **Caderas.**

Marita **¡No, no! Así.**

Murney **¡Oh! ¡Así!**

Marita **¡Ahora! A mover los brazos hacia arriba,**
hacia abajo y hacia atrás.

Murney **Los brazos**. Arms. **Hacia.** Toward.
Arriba. Up. **Abajo.** Down.
Hacia atrás. Back.

I get it. Move the arms up, down, back.
Ahora, a mover los brazos hacia arriba, hacia abajo, hacia atrás.

Marita **¡Dé una vuelta!**

Murney **¡Dé!** Give. **Una vuelta.** Oh, give a turn. Turn around! **¡Dé una vuelta! ¡Dé una vuelta!**

Marita **Doble las rodillas.**

Murney **¿Doble?** Double? Bend? Ah! **Doble. Doble las rodillas.** Knees. **Las rodillas. Las rodillas**.

Marita **Mueva los hombros.**

Murney Move. **Mueva. Mueva.**
Los hombros. The shoulders. **Los hombros.**

Marita **Estómago hacia delante. Hacia atrás.**

Murney **¡Estómago!** Stomach. **Estómago.**
Hacia delante. Toward the front.
Hacia atrás. Toward the back.
Estómago hacia delante. Hacia atrás.

Marita **Dé espalda.**
Con las manos en las caderas.

Murney **"Espalda"** is back! **Espalda.**
Dé la espalda con. With.
Con las manos en las caderas.
With your hands on the hips.
Con las manos en las caderas.

Marita **Estoy cansada.**

Murney **¿Está cansada?** You're tired? **¿Está cansada?**

Marita **Voy a descansar.**

Murney Okay. Let's rest. **Vamos a descansar.**
Let's rest. **Vamos a descansar.**
Vamos a descansar. Vamos a descansar.
Vamos a descansar.
Vamos a descansar.

Murney, Marita **Vamos a descansar.**
Vamos a descansar.

Vamos a descansar. Rest.
Vamos a descansar. Rest.
Vamos a descansar. Rest.
Vamos a descansar. Rest.

Transcript of Track 11: Relaxation

Speaker	Spoken Words
Murney	Marita, could you teach me how to relax?
Marita	**¡Oh! ¿Quiere relajarse?**
Murney	**Relajarse.** To relax yourself. **Sí, quiero relajarme.** I want. **Quiero. Relajarme.** To relax. **Quiero relajarme.**
Marita	**¿Puede escuchar música suave?**
Murney	**Puede.** You can. **Puede.** **Escuchar.** Listen. **Escuchar.** **Música.** Music. **Suave.** Soft. **Suave.** Soft. **Puede escuchar música suave.**
Marita	**Primero, tiene que acostarse boca arriba en cualquier lugar.**
Murney	First. **Primero. Primero.** **Tiene que.** You have to. **Tiene que acostarse.** To lie down. **Acostarse boca arriba.** Mouth up? Oh! We say "face up." **Boca arriba.** **En su lugar favorito. Su lugar.** Place. In your favorite place. **En su lugar favorito.**
Marita	**Va a cerrar los ojos.**
Murney	You're going to close the eyes. **Va a**. You're going to. **Cerrar.** To close. **Los ojos.** The eyes. **Va a cerrar los ojos.**
Marita	**Usted puede dejar la mente en blanco.**

Murney	You can. **Puede.** **Dejar. Puede dejar.** Leave. **Dejar.** Leave. **En blanco. La mente.** Leave the mind blank. **Usted puede dejar la mente en blanco.**
Marita	**Tiene que relajar el cuerpo.**
Murney	**Tiene que relajar.** Relax. **Relajar. El cuerpo.** **Tiene que relajar el cuerpo.**
Marita	**Inhalar por la naríz y exhalar por la boca, despacio.**
Murney	Inhale. **Inhalar. Inhalar.** Through the nose. **Por la nariz. Por la nariz.** Exhale. **Exhalar**. **Exhalar**. Through the mouth. **Por la boca. Por la boca.** **Despacio.** Slowly. **Despacio.** **Inhalar por la nariz y exhalar por la boca, despacio.**
Marita	**Inhalar profundo.**
Murney	Inhale deeply. **Inhalar profundo.** **Inhalar profundo.**
Marita	**El estómago va a moverse hacia afuera. Hacia adentro.**
Murney	**El estómago.** The stomach. **El estómago.** **Va a moverse.** Is going to move. **Mover.** **Hacia fuera.** Out. **Hacia adentro.** In. **Va a moverse hacia afuera, hacia adentro.**
Marita	**Tiene que apretar las manos y soltarlas.**
Murney	You have to.

	Apretar. Squeeze. **Apretar las manos. Tiene que apretar las manos y soltarlas. Soltar.** Let go.
Marita	**Apretar los músculos de las piernas.**
Murney	Squeeze. **Apretar. Apretar.** **Apretar los músculos.** The muscles. **Los músculos.** **De las piernas.** Of the legs. **De las piernas.** **Apretar los músculos de las piernas.**
Marita	**A mover el tobillo en círculos.**
Murney	Move the ankle. **Mover.** Move. **Mover el tobillo.** The ankle. In circles. **En círculos.** **A mover el tobillo en círculos.**
Marita	**Ahora, vamos a imaginar que está en el parque.**
Murney	Now, we are going. **Vamos a.** **Imaginar.** To imagine. **Imaginar.** **El parque.** The park. **El parque.**
Marita	**Hay arboles. ¡Mira! Las ardillas corren.**
Murney	**Hay arboles.** There are trees. **Hay arboles.** **Ardillas.** Squirrels. **Ardillas corren.** Are running.
Marita	**Un lago con patos.**
Murney	**Un lago.** Lake. **Lago.** **Con patos.** With ducks. **Con patos.**
Marita	**Rocas y cascadas.**
Murney	Rocks. **Rocas. Rocas.** **Cascadas.** Waterfalls. **Cascadas.**

Marita	**Un pequeño puente.**
Murney	A small bridge. **Puente.** Bridge. **Puente.** **Pequeño puente.** Small bridge.
Marita	**Los pajaritos cantan.**
Murney	The birds are singing. **Los pajaritos. Los pajaritos.** Birds. **Cantan.** They're singing. **Cantan.**
Marita	**Va a escuchar el sonido de las cascadas.**
Murney	**Va a escuchar.** You are going to hear. **Va a escuchar el sonido.** The sound. **El sonido.** **De las cascadas.**
Marita	**Unos señores pescan.**
Murney	Some men. **Unos señores.** **Unos señores pescan.** They're fishing. **Pescan.**
Marita	**El sol brilla.**
Murney	The sun. **El sol.** **Brilla.** Is shining. **Brilla.**
Marita	**Las nubes flotan en el cielo azul.**
Murney	The clouds. **Las nubes. Las nubes.** **Flotan en el cielo azul.** **Azul.** Blue. **Las nubes flotan en el cielo azul.**
Marita	**Puede quedarse y relajarse.**
Murney	You can stay and relax. Relax. **Puede quedarse.** You can stay. **Quedarse y relajarse.** Relax. **Relajarse.**
Marita	**Escucha la música.**
Murney	Listen to the music. **Escucha la música.** **Escucha la música.** **Escucha la música.** **Escucha la música.**

Transcript of Track 12: Daily Habits

Marita is going to have tests in the hospital.
Duerme. She is sleeping.

Speaker	Spoken Words
Murney	**Marita, tiene que despertarse.** You have to wake up. **Tiene que despertarse.**
Marita	**¿Qué hora es? ¿Es la una?**
Murney	**¿Qué hora es?** What time is it? **¡No! No es la una.** **Son las cinco.** It's five. **Son las cinco de la mañana.**
Marita	**No quiero.**
Murney	**¿No quiero?** I don't want to**. No quiero.** It's important. **Es importante. Es importante.**
Marita	**¿Por qué?**
Murney	Why? **¿Por qué?** **Va a tener exámenes en el hospital.** **Va a tener.** You're going to have. **Exámenes en el hospital.** **Exámenes en el hospital.**
Marita	**Okay. Me levanto.**
Murney	**Me levanto.** I'm getting up. **Me levanto.** **Ella.** She. **Se levanta.** Is getting up. **Ella se levanta.**
Marita	**¿Tengo que bañarme?**
Murney	Do I have to bathe myself? **¿Tengo que bañarme? ¿Tengo que bañarme?** **¡Claro!** Sure! **Ella tiene que bañarse.** She has to bathe herself. **Tiene que bañarse.**

Marita **Tengo hambre.**

Murney You cannot eat. **No puede comer. No puede comer.**

Marita **¿Un café o leche?**

Murney **Ni leche.** Milk. **Leche. Ni café.**
Tiene que tener el estómago vacío.
El estómago. The stomach.
Vacío. Empty.

Tiene que. You have to.
Tener el estómago vacío.

Marita **¿Cuándo puedo comer?**

Murney **¿Cuándo?** When? **¿Puedo comer?** Can I eat?
¿Cuando puedo comer?

Después del examen.
After the exam. After the test.
Después del examen.

Marita **Voy a morir de hambre.**

Murney **Voy a morir.** I'm going to die. **Voy a morir.**
De hambre. Of hunger.

Favor de ponerse la ropa.
Do me the favor of putting on your clothes.
Favor de ponerse la ropa.
Ponerse la ropa.

Marita **Está bien. Déme tiempo.**

Murney **Está bien.** Okay.
Déme. Give me.
Give me time. **Déme tiempo. Déme tiempo.**

¿Lista? ¿Está lista? Are you ready?
¡Vámonos!

Transcript of Track 13: Fire

Important: If you are a first responder, also study tracks 5, 6, and 7.

We've just received an emergency call. There's a fire in an apartment building. We're on the way to the scene. It's summer, and many children are at home. Some are alone.

Speaker	Spoken Words
Fireman	We are arriving at the apartments. We've got to clear the building. Murney, I need you to go from door to door; notify the people.
Murney	Marita! Please come with me! **Favor de acompañarme.** **Acompañarme.** Accompany me. **Favor de acompañarme.**
Marita	**Oigo a un bebé llorando**.
Murney	You hear a baby crying? **¿Oye?** You hear? **¿A un bebé?** A baby! **¿Llorando?** Crying? **¡A un bebé llorando!**
Marita	**Toco la puerta y no contestan**.
Murney	You're knocking? **¿Toca? ¿Toca?** **¿Y nadie?** No one? **Contesta.** No one answers! **¡Nadie contesta!**
Marita	**Finalmente alguien contestó. ¡Gracias a Dios!**
Murney	**¡Ah! ¡Gracias a Dios!** Thank God! **¡Gracias a Dios!** **Finalmente.** Finally. **Alguien.** Someone. Answered. **Contestó.** **Alguien contestó.**

Someone answered. **Alguien contestó.**

Marita **¡Afuera! ¡Afuera!**
¡Fuego! ¡Encendio!

Murney **¡Afuera!** Out! **¡Afuera!**
¡Fuego! Fire! **¡Fuego! ¡Encendio!**

¡Por favor afuera! ¡No elevador!
¡Por la escalera! ¡Por la escalera!
The stairs. **Por la escalera.**

Marita **Abra la puerta, por favor. Mucho humo.**

Murney **¡Abra la puerta, por favor**!
Open! **¡Abra!**
Abra la puerta. Puerta. Door.
Abra la puerta, por favor.

Fireman **¡Soy bombera! ¡Tiene que salir!**

Murney **Bombera.** Firefighter. **Soy.** I am.
Soy bombera. I'm a firefighter.

¡Tiene que salir! You have to leave!
¡Tiene que! You have to. **Salir. ¡Tiene que salir!**

Marita **¡Un jardín de niños! Muchos niños.**

Murney **¡Ay!** A day care! **¡Un jardín de niños!**
Muchos niños. Many children. **Muchos niños.**

Marita **Respire profundo y favor de calmarse.**
Respire profundo.

Fireman I said everyone out!

Murney Breathe deeply. **Respire.** Breathe.
Profundo. Deeply. **Hondo.** Deeply.
Respire hondo.

Favor de calmarse.
Do me the favor of calming yourself.
¡Favor de calmarse!

Marita	**Hay mucho humo. ¡Cuidado!**
Murney	**Hay.** There is. **Humo.** Smoke. **¡Hay humo!** Be careful! **¡Cuidado! ¡Cuidado!**
Marita	**¿Todos están afuera y a salvo?**
Murney	**¿Todos?** Everyone? **¿Está afuera?** Is outside? **Todos están afuera.** **Y a salvos.** Safe! **¡Salvos!**
Marita	**Todos tienen que ir al médico.**
Murney	**Todos.** Everyone. **Todos tienen que ir.** They all have to go. **Ir al médico.** **Tienen que ir al médico.** **Todos tienen que ir.**
Marita	**Todo terminó.**
Murney	Everything is over. **Ya terminó.**

What you heard in the background was:

- **¡Socorro!** Help! **¡Socorro!**
- **¡Mucho humo!** Much smoke! **¡Mucho humo!**
- Everybody out! **¡Todos afuera!**

Earlier you heard:

- **¡No elevador! ¡No elevador!** Not the elevator!
- **¡Por la escalera! ¡Por la escalera!** By the stairs.

Transcript of Track 14: Emotions

Julia [pronounced Who-Leah] ("Julia" in English) awoke to barking in the night. She went to the kitchen and saw her boyfriend hitting the dog. She was afraid. In the morning she called her friend, Murney.

Speaker	**Spoken Words**
Julia	**Lo siento por llamar tan temprano.** **Tengo miedo.**
Murney	**¿Tiene miedo?** You have fear? **¿Tiene miedo?** You're afraid? **¿Tiene miedo?** **Lo siento.** I'm sorry. **¿Lo siente?** You're sorry about it? **¿Lo siente?** **¿Por llamar?** For calling? **¿Tan temprano?** **¿Lo siente por llamar tan temprano?** So early? **¿Tan temprano?**
Julia	**Me dice que no va a hacerlo otra vez.**
Murney	**Le dice.** He tells you. **Le dice.** **Que no va.** He's not going. **¿No va a hacerlo?** To do it? **¿Otra vez? ¿No va a hacerlo otra vez?**
Julia	**No confío en él.**
Murney	**¿No confía?** You don't trust? **¿En él? ¿No confía en él?** Julia, you're the next person he's going to hit! **Usted es.** You are. The next person. **La próxima persona.** **Que él va a golpear.** That he's going to hit. **¡Ya voy a su casa!** I'm going to your house. **Ya voy a su casa.**

	[Knocking at the door]
Speaker	**Spoken Words**
Tommy	Who is it?
Julia	**Mi hija tiene moretones por todo el cuerpo. No puede ser.**
Murney	**¿Su hija?** Your daughter? **¿Tiene? ¿Su hija tiene moretones?** She has bruises. **¿Por todo el cuerpo?** All over her body? **Su hija tiene moretones por todo el cuerpo.** **¡No puede ser! ¡No puede ser!** **Sí, puede ser.** It can be! **Sí, puede ser.**
Julia	**Si esto es cierto, voy a hacer un reporte.**
Murney	If that's true. **¿Si esto es cierto?** If it's certain. **Si esto es cierto.** **Va a hacer.** You are going to make. **¿Va a hacer un reporte?** A report? **¿Va a hacer un reporte?** **Está en pelígro.** You're in danger. **¡Está en pelígro!**
Julia	**¡Mariana! ¡Mariana!**
Mariana	**¡Ya voy!** I'm coming. **¡Ya voy!**
Julia	**¡Mariana! ¡Déjame chequearte!**
Murney	**Déjame.** Let me. **Chequearte.** Check you. **Déjame chequearte.**

Chapter 6: Using Questionnaires

Important: The English words are given with the Spanish words so that you can easily acquire the vocabulary by using each questionnaire.

Conduct an Intake Examination

Tomar Signos Vitales—Take Vital Signs

Es necesario It is necessary	**tomarle** to take	**los signos vitales.** your vital signs.
Voy a I am going	**tomarle** to take	**la temperatura.** your temperature.
Voy a I am going	**tomarle** to take	**la presión.** your blood pressure.
Voy a I am going	**tomarle** to take	**el pulso.** your pulse.
Favor de Do the favor of	**darme** giving me	**la mano.** your hand.
Favor de Do the favor of	**quitarse** taking off	**la ropa de la cintura para arriba.** the clothes from the waist up.

(Skip the following sentence if you are the doctor.)

Esperar Wait for	**al médico** the doctor	**aquí.** here.

Primeras Preguntas—Initial Questions

Soy el médico. Soy el Doctor ______________.
Soy la Doctora ______________.
I am the doctor. I am Dr. ___________________.

Voy a	**hacerle**	**unas preguntas.**
I am going to	make (ask)	some questions.

Después,	**voy a**	**examinarle.**
Afterward,	I am going to	examine you.

¿Qué pasó? What happened? ______________________________

¿Cuándo? When? ____

¿Qué le duele? What is hurting you?

____

Favor de	**mostrar**	**dónde le duele.**
Do the favor of	showing	where it hurts.

Pedir Permiso—Ask Permission

Show respect for the patient with the following statement and question.

Me gustaría	**hacerle**	**un reconocimiento físico.**
I would like	to do	a complete physical examination.

¿Me permite?
Do you permit me?

The patient will answer, **"Sí."**
La Cabeza—The Head

Favor de	**doblar la cabeza**	**hacia adelante.**
Do the favor of	turning your head	toward forward.

Favor de	**doblar la cabeza**	**hacia atrás.**
Do the favor of	turning your head	toward back.

Favor de	**doblar la cabeza**	**la izquierda.**
Do the favor of	turning your head	toward to the left.

Favor de	**doblar la cabeza**	**la derecha.**
Do the favor of	turning your head	toward to the right.

Los Ojos—The Eyes

Favor de	**abrir**	**los ojos.**
Do me the favor	of opening	the eyes.

Voy a	**examinarle**	**con esta luz.**
I am going	to examine	with this light.

Favor de	**mirar hacia**	**arriba.**
Do me the favor of	looking toward	above.

Favor de	**mirar hacia**	**abajo.**
Do me the favor of	looking toward	below.

La Boca—The Mouth

Favor de	**abrir**	**la boca.**
Do the favor of	opening	the mouth.

Decir	**¡ah!**
Say	ah!

Sacar	**la lengua.**
Stick out	the tongue.

La Nariz—The Nose

¿Puede	**respirar bien**	**con la nariz?**
Can you	breathe well	with the nose?

¿Algún desecho? Some discharge?

El Torax—The Thorax

¿Hay	**dolor**	**del pecho?**
Is there	pain	in the chest?

¿Le duele	**cuando**	**palpo aquí?**
Does it hurt	when	I touch here?

Favor de	**respirar/inhalar**	**hondo.**
Do the favor of	breathing/inhaling	deeply.

Otra vez. Again.

Es necesario	**aguantar**	**la respiración.**
It is necessary	to hold	the breath.

Favor de	**exhalar.**
Do the favor of	exhaling.

El Corazón—The Heart

Voy a	**escuchar**	**el corazón.**
I am going	to listen to	your heart.

El Abdomen—The Abdomen

Favor de	**acostarse**	**boca arriba.**
Do the favor of	lying down	mouth up (face up).
Voy a	**examinarle**	**el abdomen.**
I am going	to examine	the abdomen.

¿Le duele aquí?
Does it hurt here?

¿Le duele más aquí?
Does it hurt more here?

Favor de	**levantarse**	**ahora.**
Do the favor of	getting up	now.

Eso es todo.
That is all.

El Examen Pélvico—The Pelvic Exam

Voy a	**examinarle**	**por dentro.**
I am going to	examine you	internally.
Favor de	**poner los pies**	**en los estribos**.
Do the favor of	putting the feet	in the stirrups.
¿Es posible	**relajarse?**	
Is it possible	to relax yourself?	
No le	**va a**	**doler.**
It is not	going to	hurt (you).

Voy a	**hacerle**	**la prueba**	**Papanicolaou.**
I am going	to do	the test	Pap smear.

Eso es todo.	**Gracias.**
That is all!	Thanks.

El Examen del Recto—The Rectal Exam

Voy a	**examinarle**	**el recto.**	
I am going	to examine	the rectum.	
Es posible	**relajarse?**		
Is it possible to relax?			
Favor de	**acostarse**	**al lado derecho.**	
Do the favor of	lying down	on your right side.	
Favor de	**acostarse**	**al lado izquierdo.**	
Do the favor of	lying down	on your left side.	
¿Es posible/Es necesario		**doblar las piernas?**	
Is it possible/Is it necessary		to bend your legs?	
Voy a	**introducir**	**mi dedo**	**con el guante.**
I am going	to insert	my finger	with the glove.

Termine el Examen—End the Exam

Está bien.
That is good.

Eso es todo por hoy.
That is all for today.

Take a Clinical History

Interview with a Form (Entrevista con formulario)

Fecha (Date) ______________________________

Nombre del Paciente ______________________________
(Name of patient)

Edad (Age) ______________________________

Favor de contester las preguntas con una marca (x) o frase.
Please answer the questions with a mark (x) or a phrase.

Queja principal (Main complaint)

____

____

Salud (Health, General Health)

¿Cómo es su salud en general? (How is your general health?)

Buena (Good) ___ **Regular** (Regular) ___ **Mala** (Bad) ___

¿Cuándo fue la última vez que se sintió bien? ____________
(When was the last time that you felt well?)

¿Cambio de peso? (Change in weight?) ____________________

¿Cuánto pesa? (How much do you weigh?) __________________

¿Cuánto pesaba? (How much did you weigh?) ______________

¿Duerme bien? (Do you sleep well?) _______________________

¿Hace ejercicio? (Do you exercise?) _______________________

¿Cada día? (Each day?) ___ **¿Cada semana?** (Each week?) ____

¿Qué hace en su tiempo libre? (What do you do in your free time?)

____

____

____

____

Cirugías (Surgeries)

Operación (Operation) **Lugar** (Place) **Fecha** (Date)

____

____

____

____

El Sistéma Respiratorio (The Respiratory System)

Ha sufrido de …? (Have you suffered from …?)

- **¿Pulmonia?** (pneumonia) sí___ no___
- **¿Bronquitis?** (bronchitis) sí___ no___
- **¿Pleuresía?** (pleurisy) sí___ no___
- **¿Tuberculosis?** (tuberculosis) sí___ no___
- **¿Asma?** (asthma) sí___ no___
- **¿Bronquitis crónica?** (chronic bronchitis) sí___ no___
- **¿Enfisema?** (emphysema) sí___ no___
- **¿Otro?** (another illness) sí___ no___

  ¿Cuál? (which) ______________

El Sistéma Digestivo (The Digestive System)

¿Ha tenido o tiene …? (Have you had or do you have …?)

- **¿Dificultad en tragar?** (difficulty swallowing) sí____no___
- **¿Ardor en el pecho?** (burning in chest) sí____no___
- **¿Reflujo de comida?** (reflux) sí____no___
- **¿Náusea o vómito?** (nausea or vomiting) sí____no___
- **¿Dolor abdominal?** (abdominal pain) sí____no___
- **¿Estreñemiento?** (constipation) sí____no___
- **¿Dificultad en hacer popo?** (difficulty in making poop)
  sí____no___
- **¿Diarrea?** (diarrhea) sí____no___

¿Ha tenido cambio de …? (Have you had a change in …?)

- **¿Apetito?** (appetite) sí____no___
- **¿Excrementos (popo)?** (excrement) sí____no___
- **¿Consistencia de popo?** (consistency) sí____no___

¿Ha sufrido de o sufre de …? (Have you suffered from or do you suffer from …?)

- **¿Ulceras**? (ulcers) sí____no___
- **¿Hernia hiatal?** (hiatal hernia) sí____no___
- **¿Hernia de esófago?** (esophageal hernia) sí____no___
- **¿Excrementos (popos) negros?** sí____no___
  (black stool)

¿Problema? (Problem)

Tiene problema de …? (Have you had a problema with …?)

- **¿Hígado?** (liver) sí____no___
- **¿Vesicular?** (gallbladder) sí____no___
- **¿Cálculos?** (gallstones) sí____no___
- **¿Páncreas?** (pancreas) sí____no___
- **¿Diarreas?** (diarrhea) sí____no___
- **¿Colitis o disentería?** sí____no___
  (colitis or dysentery)
- **¿Diverticulitis?** (diverticulitis) sí____no___
- **¿Sangre en el excremento (popo)?** sí____no___
  (blood in the feces)
- **¿Hemorroides?** (hemorrhoids) sí____no___
- **¿Hernia?** (hernia) sí____no___

Radiografías (X-rays)

¿Ha tenido radiografías de …? (Have you had X-rays of …?)

- **¿El estómago (serie gastrointestinal)?** sí____no___
  (the stomach [gastrointestinal series])
- **¿La vesicular?** (vesicular) sí____no___
- **¿Colon? (bario enema)** sí____no___
  (colon [barium enema])

Dificultades (Difficulties)

¿Tiene dificultades con …? (Do you have difficulties with …?)

- **¿Disco vertebral?** (vertebral disc) sí____no___
- **¿Nervio ciático?** (sciatic nerve) sí____no___
- **¿Gota?** (gout) sí____no___
- **¿Reumatismo?** (rheumatism) sí____no___
- **¿Artritis?** (arthritis) sí____no___
- **¿Hinchazón de las coyunturas?** sí____no___
  (swelling of the joints)
- **¿Vías urinarias?** (urinary tract) sí____no___

¿Tiene …? Do you have …?

- **¿Enfermedad de los riñones?** sí____no___
  (kidney disease)
- **¿Proteína e la orina?** sí____no___
  (protein in the urine)
- **¿Sangre o pus en la orina?** sí____no___
  (blood or pus in the urine)
- **¿Piedras o cálculos en los riñones?** sí____no___
  (stones or calculus in the kidneys)
- **¿Enfermedad de la vejiga?** sí____no___
  (bladder disease)
- **¿Problemas de la próstata?** sí____no___
  (prostate problems)

Historia Obstétrica y Ginecológica (Obstetric and Gynecologic History)

¿Tiene …? Do you have …?

- **¿Tumores?** (tumors) sí____no___
- **¿Quistes?** (pron. *key-ss-tays*) (cysts) sí____no___
- **¿Problemas con las glándulas mamarias (senos)?** (problems with breasts) sí____no___

¿Ha tenido …? Have you had …?

- **¿Embarazos?** (pregnancies) sí____no___
- **¿Abortos terapéuticos?** (therapeutic abortions) sí____no___
- **¿Pérdidas?** (losses, spontaneous abortions) sí____no___
- **¿Sangre entre períodos?** (bleeding between periods) sí____no___
- **¿Toxemia?** (toxemia) sí____no___

¿Cuándo fue la última regla? ____________
(When was the last menstrual cycle?)

¿Cuántos días dura la regla? ____________
(How many days does the period last?)

¿Son regulares? (Are they regular?) sí____no___

¿Histerectomía? (A hysterectomy?) sí____no___

¿Círugia de los órganos femeninos? sí____no___
(Surgery on the female organs?)

Neurológica (Neurological)

¿Sufre de ...? (Do you suffer from ...?)

- **¿Dolor de cabeza?** (headaches) sí____no___
  ¿Frecuentamente? (frequently) sí____no___
- **¿Convulsiones?** (convulsions) sí____no___
  ¿Frecuentamente? (frequently) sí____no___
- **¿Enfermedad neurológica?** sí____no___
  (neurological illness)
- **¿Embolia?** (clot, embolism) sí____no___
- **¿Parálisis?** (paralysis) sí____no___

¿Tiene dificultad de ...? (Dou you have difficulty of ...?)

- **¿Coordinar?** (coordination) sí____no___
- **¿Movimiento?** (movement) sí____no___
- **¿Caminar?** (walking) sí____no___
- **¿Hablar?** (speaking) sí____no___
- **¿Visión doble?** (double vision) sí____no___
- **¿Alucinaciones?** (hallucinations) sí____no___

¿Colapso nervioso? (nervous breakdown)

____

¿Depresión? (depression)

____

¿Enfermedad psiquiátrica? (psychiatric illness)

____

Ojos (Eyes)

¿Cirugía de la vista? (eye surgery) sí____no___

¿Glaucoma? (glaucoma) sí____no___

Oídos (Ears)

¿Sordera? (deafness) sí____no___

¿Ruidos anormales en los oídos? sí____no___
(abnormal noises in the ears)

¿Zumbidos? (ringing) sí____no___

Alergías (allergies)

¿Tiene ...?

- **¿Alergias communes?** sí____no___
  (common allergies)
- **¿Al polvo?** (to dust) sí____no__
- **Al pólen?** (to pollen) sí____no___
- **¿Fiebre de heno?** (hay fever) sí____no___
- **¿Asma?** (asthma) sí____no___
- **¿Ronchas or erupciones de la piel?** sí____no___
  (rashes or hives)
- **¿Alergía a alguna medicina?** sí____no___
  (allergies to medicine)
- **¿A la penicilina?** (to penicillin) sí____no___
- **¿Picazón?** (itching) sí____no___
- **¿Hinchazón?** (swelling) sí____no___

Sleep Disorder History—Trastornos del Sueño

Note: You know that the “he/she” form of the verb can refer to usted.

Estar desvelado = to be sleep deprived.

- Él (he) está desvelado.
- Ella (she) está desvelada.

Algunas preguntas acerca del insomnio (desvelo):
Some questions about sleeplessness:

Acerca del sueño:
About sleep:

¿Cómo duerme? ______ **bien** ______ **mal**
How does he/she sleep? well badly

¿Cuánto duerme? ______ **horas**
How much does he/she sleep? hours

¿Ronca? sí____no___
Does he/she snore?

¿Hay episodios cuando no respire mientras duerme?
Are there episodes when he/she does not breathe while sleeping?
sí____no___

Estado Emocional: Emotional State

¿Está deprimido? sí____no___
Is he/she depressed?

¿Está ansioso sí____no___
Is he/she anxious?

¿O se siente estresado? sí____no___
Or is he/she feeling stressed?

¿Está aburrido? sí____no___
Is he/she bored?

Desarrollo del Niño: Development of the Child

Cuándo	**puede**	**caminar?**	_____**meses** ___**años**
When	is he/she able	to walk?	months years

El crecimiento normal de los niños puede dividirse en areas:
The normal growth of children can be divided into areas:

Habilidad Motora: Motor Skills

Controlar la cabeza (control of the head) _____meses _____años
Sentarse (to sit up by self) _____meses _____años
Caminar (to walk) _____meses _____años

Habilidad Motora Primaria: Early Motor Skills

Sostener una cuchara (to hold a spoon) ____ meses _____años

Sujetar un pedazo de cereal con un dedo y el dedo pulgar
(to hold a piece of cereal with a finger and the thumb)
______meses _____años

Sensorial (Los Sentidos): The Senses

Ver (to see) _____meses _____años
Escuchar (to listen) _____meses _____años
Saborear (to taste) _____meses _____años
Tocar (to touch) _____meses _____años
Oler (to smell) _____meses _____años

Lenguaje: Language

Ser capaz de hablar y hacerse entender _____meses _____años
(to be able to speak and make self understood)

Comprender lo que dicen los padres u otros niños
(to understand what parents or other children say)
_____meses _____años

Habilidad Social: Social Skill

Habilidad para jugar con los familiares y con otros niños
(ability to play with relatives and with other children)
_____meses _____años

Chapter 7: Explaining Procedures

Important: The English words are below the Spanish words so that you can easily acquire the vocabulary by using each explanation.

Cardiology Procedure—Procedimiento Cardíaco

Los riesgos de complicaciones serias con el procedimiento …
The risks of serious complications with the procedure …
… son muy bajos.
… are very low.

Son menos de un porcentaje de los siguientes incidencias.
They are less than one percent of the following incidents.

No hay mucha probabilidad de hemorragia …
There is not much probability of hemorrhage …
… que requiere transfusión de sangre.
… that requires transfusion of blood.

El promedio de pérdida de sangre es menos de …
The average of loss of blood is less than …
… una o dos cucharaditas.
… one or two teaspoons.

La infección es muy rara porque usamos técnicas esteriles …
Infection is rare because we use sterile techniques …
… como el uso de gorros, mascaras, y camisones …
… such as the use of caps, masks, and gowns …
… durante el procedimiento.
… during the procedure.

El catéter puede tocar la pared del corazón y causar …
The catheter can touch the wall of the heart and cause …
… **un ritmo anormal del corazón.**
… an abnormal rhythm of the heart.

El ritmo usualmente se pone normal cuando se quita el catéter.
The rhythm usually becomes normal when the catheter is removed.

Rara vez, tenemos que dar medicina o electricidad
Rarely, we have to give medicine or electricity
… para ponerse normal el ritmo.
… to put in place a normal rhythm.

El catéter **puede perforar por** **la pared** **del corazón.**
The catheter can puncture the wall of the heart.

Pero es improbable **porque** **los catéteres** **son muy suaves.**
But it is unlikely because the catheters are very soft.

Hay un riesgo **de daño a la arteria que puede causar …**
There is a risk of damage to the artery that can cause …
… un pulso débil **en el pie.**
… a weak pulse in the foot.

Si vemos esto, **podemos empezar una medicina …**
If we see this, we can start a medicine …
… para disminuir coágulos de sangre en la pierna…
… to decrease blood clots in the leg…
… puede causar un pulso débil.
… that can cause a weak pulse.

Hay un riesgo **de un coágulo** **de sangre** **en el catéter.**
There is a risk of a clot of blood in the catheter.

El coágulo puede romperse, viajar al cerebro, y causar …
The clot can break off, travel to the brain, and cause …
… un derrame cerebral.
… a stroke.

Es improbable porque damos medicina para prevenir …
This is unlikely because we give medicine to prevent …
… que coágulos de sangre se forman durante el procedimiento.
… that clots of blood are formed during the procedure.

Hay un riesgo de daño a la válvula del corazón …
There is a risk of damage to the valve of the heart …
… o a la pared del sanguíneo.
… or to the wall of the blood vessel.

Con el globo que se infla, hay un riesgo de colocar …
With the balloon that is inflated, there is a risk of placing …
… el aparato/espiral/stent en el lugar equivocado.
… the device/coil/stent in the wrong position.

También el aparato/espiral/stent puede moverse a …
Also the device/coil/stent can move to …

… otra parte del cuerpo.
… another part of the body.

Usualmente se puede quitar el aparato/espíral/stent …
Usually one can remove the device/coil/stent …

… con un catéter especial llamado un snare.
… with a special catheter called a snare.

Además, hay siempre un riesgo pequeño de ataque cardíaco …
Moreover, there is always a small risk of cardiac arrest …

… y la necesidad de resucitación cardiopulmonar.
… and the necessity for CPR.

Tambien hay siempre un riesgo pequeño de la muerte ...
Also there is always a very small risk of death …

… con cualquier procedimiento que hacemos.
… with any procedure we do.

Notes:
There is no translation for "stent" other than a description, such as "a metal tube" ("un tubo alámbrico").

There is no translation for "snare" other than the description "a special catheter" ("un catéter especial").

Explain a Pelvic Ultrasound Exam

El ultrasonido (o ecografía) hace uso …
The ultrasound makes use of …
… de las ondas de sonido con alta frecuencia.
… waves of sound (sound waves) with high frequency.

Las ondas **hacen un eco** **en las estructoras** **del cuerpo.**
The waves make an echo in the structures of the body.

Una computadora **recibe** **las ondas reflejadas …**
A computer receives the reflected waves …
… para crear **una imagen.**
… to create an image.

Es posible **observar** **los órganos** **y estructuras …**
It is possible to observe the organs and structures …
… dentro **del cuerpo.**
… inside of the body.

Profesionales **de la salud** **usan el ultrasonido …**
Professionals of health use the ultrasound …
… para ver **el corazón.**
… to see the heart.

Durante el embarazo, **los médicos** **usan las pruebas** …
During the pregnancy, the doctors use the tests …
… para examinar el feto dentro **del cuerpo.**
… in order to examine the fetus inside of the body.

La ecografía **no tiene** **el riesgo de exposición** **a la radiación.**
The ultrasound does not have the risk of exposure to radiation.

El examen se hace **en la sala de** **ecografías** **o de radiología.**
The exam is done in the room of ultrasound or of radiology.

El paciente se acuesta.
The patient lies down.

Un gel conductor **(claro a base de agua)** **se aplica …**
A conductive gel (clear with a water base) is applied …
… en el área **del cuerpo** **que se va a evaluar.**
… on the area of the body that will be evaluated.

Una sonda manual **se pone en** **el area.**
A manual probe is put on the area.

El gel	**se siente**	**un poco frío.**
The gel	feels	a bit cold

Give Patient Instructions before Anesthesia

Please	Instruction
Favor de …	**Acostarse boca abajo.** Lie down on your stomach, please.
	Acostarse boca arriba. Lie down on your back, please.
	Acostarse al lado izquierdo. Lie down on your left side, please.
	Sentarse/levantarse. Sit down/get up, please.
	No moverse. Don't move, please. (Note: no + verb = don't *verb*)
	Respirar muy hondo/profundo/profundamente. Breathe deeply, please.
	Doblar la rodilla. Bend the knee, please.
	Ponerse las rodillas al pecho. Bring the knees to the chest, please.
	Voltearse/darse vuelta Turn over, please.
	Contar a diez, lentamente. Count to ten, slowly.

Take X-Rays of the Arm

(Sacar radiografías del brazo)

Voy a	**sacar/tomar**	**un rayo-X**	**del brazo.**
I am going	to take	an X-ray	of your arm.

Quiero saber	**si**	**está roto.**
I want to know	if	it is broken.

El paciente	**tiene que**	**quitar**	**su camisa.**
The patient	has to	take off	his shirt.

Tiene que/va a	**pararse**	**delante de la máquina.**
He has to/is going to	stand	in front of the machine.

La prueba	**no va**	**a durar mucho.**
The test	is not going	to take long.

El líquido	**sabe mal/está mal.**
The liquid	tastes bad/is bad.

Usted tiene	**un tumor**	**en el sistema digestivo.**
You have	a tumor	in your digestive tract.

Tengo	**calambres muy fuertes.**
I have	very strong cramps.

Me duele	**con presión**	**en el estómago**.
It hurts	with pressure	on my stomach.

¿Va a	**quitar**	**el tumor?**
Are you going	to remove	the tumor?

Take Gallbladder X-Rays

(Sacar radiografías de la vesícula biliar)

El médico **piensa** **que tengo**
The doctor thinks that I have
cálculos biliares (cálculos de biliar).
gallstones.

Va a **operar pronto.**
He is going to operate soon.

Dice **que voy a** **tener nausea**
He says that I'm going to have nausea
después de las pruebas.
after the tests.

Va a **examinar los resultados** **de las pruebas.**
He is going to examine the results of the X-rays.

¿Voy a **estar muy débil?**
Am I going to be very weak?

Nuclear Scan of Liver and Gallbladder

(Exploración nuclear del hígado y de la vesícla biliar)

Hay **anormalidades** **en el hígado.**
There are abnormalities in my liver.

Examinó **la vesicular biliar.**
He examined my gallbladder.

La máquina **registra la señal.**
The machine picks up the signal.

Hay **una máquina especial** **que saca/toma fotos.**
There is a special machine that makes pictures.

Nuclear Scan of Pancreas

(Exploración nuclear del páncreas)

Tengo	**quistes**	**en el pancreas.**
I have	cysts	in my pancreas

¿Por qué	**inyecta materia radioactivo**	**en el brazo?**
Why	does he inject radioactive material	in my arm?

¿Va a ser	**peligroso**	**el procedimiento?**
Is it going to be	a dangerous	procedure?

Había	**una reacción alérgica.**
There was (*había* = past of *hay*)	an allergic reaction.

Una cámara especial	**saca fotos**	**del [de + el = del] páncreas.**
A special camera	takes pictures	of my pancreas.

Collect Urine with Catheter

(Colleccionar la orina con un catéter)

Van a sacar	**la orina**	**de la vejiga.**
They are going to remove	the urine	from the bladder.

El catéter	**va a**	**estar incómodo (irritar).**
The catheter	is going	to be uncomfortable (to irritate).

Yo sé	**que voy a tener**	**el riesgo de infección.**
I know	that I am running	the risk of infection.

¿Voy a	**tener**	**mucho dolor?**	**(Me va a**	**doler mucho?)**
Am I going	to have	a lot of pain?	(Is it going	to hurt me much?)

¿Cómo	**vamos a evitar**	**las complicaciones?**
How are	we going to avoid	complications?

Intravenous Pyelogram

(El pielograma intravenoso)

Inyectó	**yodo en el brazo.**	
He injected	iodine dye into my arm.	
Dice que	**tengo/sufro de**	**las piedras nefríticas.**
He says that	I have/I suffer from	kidney stones.
Sacó	**rayos-X**	**de los riñones.**
He took	X-rays	of my kidneys.
Trata de	**curar al paciente.**	
He is trying	to cure the patient.	

Chapter 8: Written Practice

El (masculine)	La (feminine)
El doctor (the male doctor)	La doctora (the female doctor)
El médico (the male doctor)	La médica (the female doctor)
El especialista (the specialist)	La especialista (the specialist)
El técnico (the male technician)	La técnica (the female technician)
El terapéuta (the male therapist)	La terapéuta (the female therapist)
El enfermero (the male nurse)	La enfermera (the female nurse)
Los enfermeros (male nurses or male and female nurses)	Las enfermas (the female nurses)
El partero (the male midwife)	La partera (the female midwife)
El paciente (the male patient)	La paciente (the female patient)
El bebé (the male baby)	La bebé (the female baby)
El niño (the boy child)	La niña (the girl child)
El joven (the young man)	La joven (the young lady)
El hijo (the son)	La hija (the daughter)
El nene (the baby boy, informal)	La nena (the baby girl, informal)
-	La clínica (the clinic)
-	La oficina (the office)
El hospital (the hospital)	-
El exámen (the examination)	La prueba (the test)
El análisis (the analysis)	El diagnosis (the diagnosis)

The Body

The Head (La Cabeza)—Written Practice

Use the preceding table and the word bank below to translate and write each sentence in Spanish. Note: The Spanish answers are on the next page.

Word Bank

hacer = to make
hacer = to do
según = according to
disgustado = upset
está = is temporarily
es = is permanently
el análices = analysis

1. The patient is going to leave the hospital tomorrow.
2. The technician is going to do the analyses in the laboratory.
3. The patient in room thirty-two is **(está)** very upset.
4. The man has a pain in his left ear.
5. The child is going to the hospital at eight.
6. How long have you had the pain?
7. What are you going to do for your sore throat?
8. According to the doctor, the condition is not **(no está)** serious.
9. The nurse is going to come now.
10. According to **(según)** the therapist, I have to do exercises.
11. My son has a pain in his right eye.
12. We are going to believe that he is going to tell the truth.
13. According to the specialist, an operation is **(es)** necessary.
14. When are you going to leave the hospital?

The Head (La Cabeza)—Answers

Note: Feel free to mix and match the phrases.

1. **El paciente** **va a salir** **del hospital mañana.**
   The patient is going to leave the hospital tomorrow.
2. **El técnico** **va a hacer** **el análisis** **en el laboratorio.**
   The technician is going to do the analyses in the laboratory.
3. **El paciente** **en el cuarto treinta y dos** **está muy disgustado.**
   The patient in room thirty-two is very upset.
4. **El hombre** **tiene un dolor** **en el oído izquierdo.**
   The man has a pain in his left ear.
5. **El niño** **va a al hospital** **a las ocho.**
   The child is going to the hospital at eight.
6. **¿Hace cuánto** **tiene** **el dolor?**
   How long have you had the pain?
7. **¿Qué va a hacer** **para el** **dolor de garganta?**
   What are you going to do for your sore throat?
8. **Según el médico,** **la condición no está muy grave/seria.**
   According to the doctor, the condition is not very serious.
9. **La enfermera** **va a venir** **ahora.**
   The nurse is going to come now.
10. **Según el terapéuta,** **tengo que hacer** **ejercicios.**
    According to the therapist, I have to do exercises.
11. **Mi hijo** **tiene un dolor** **en el ojo derecho.**
    My son has a pain in his right eye.
12. **Vamos a creer que** **va a** **decir la verdad.**
    We are going to believe that he is going to tell the truth.
13. **Según el especialista,** **una operación** **es necesaria.**
    According to the specialist, an operation is necessary.
14. **¿Cuándo** **va a salir** **del hospital?**
    When are you going to leave the hospital?

Head Examination (Examen de la Cabeza)—Written Practice

Note: The Spanish answers appear at the end.

Doctor	Where does it hurt, Mr./Mrs.?	
Patient	The throat hurts me.	
Doctor	Please shirt. It is necessary	sit and take off your to put on the gown.
Patient	Good.	
Doctor	It is necessary Do you have	to breathe deeply. a cough?
Patient	Yes, for __days or __ weeks.	
Doctor	Please open your mouth. Please stick out your tongue.	
Patient	What is happening?	
Doctor	You have a virus. It is necessary to take an antibiotic.	

Head Examination (Examen de la Cabeza)—Answers

Note: You can mix and match the phrases as you become proficient.

Médico/Médica	**¿Dónde le duele, señor/señora?** Where does it hurt, Mr./Mrs.?	
Paciente	**Me duele la garganta.** The throat hurts me.	
Médico/Médica	**Favor de** Please	**sentarse y quitarse la camisa.** sit and take off the shirt.
	Es necesario It is necessary	**ponerse el camisón.** to put on the gown.
Paciente	**Bien.** Good.	
Médico/Médica	**Es necesario** It is necessary	**respirar profundamente.** to breathe deeply.
	¿Tiene Do you have	**tos?** a cough?
Paciente	**Sí, __días, __semanas.** Yes, __days, __weeks.	
Médico/Médica	**Favor de** Please	**abrir la boca.** open the mouth.
	Favor de Please	**sacar la lengua.** stick out the tongue.
Paciente	**¿Qué pasa?** What is happening?	
Médico/Médica	**Usted tiene un virus.** You have a virus.	
	Es necesario tomar un antibiotico. It is necessary to take an antibiotic.	

The Trunk (El Tronco)—Written Practice

Translate the following statements and questions into written Spanish. The underlined words are phrases you learned in Table 3, "The Torso—El Tronco," in chapter 4.

1. I have had a pain in my chest for an hour.
2. She has been suffering from headaches for two months.
3. The male nurse has to bathe the patient.
4. The specialist is going to examine the patient.
5. The female doctor is going to prescribe/give pills.
6. The male technician is going to take an X-ray of my chest.
7. I don't like to exercise.
8. He is afraid of the hospital.
9. The female nurse wants to learn Spanish.
10. I wish to speak with the receptionist.
11. The male patient has to go to the clinic today.
12. He is in pain, and he is very nervous.
13. She has to take more tests.
14. My mother has to stay in the hospital for a week.
15. The male doctor is going to make a diagnosis.

Word Bank

hacer = to make	**nervioso** = nervous
recetar = to prescribe	**los exámenes** = the tests
bañarle = to bathe someone	**el análisis** = the analysis
venir = to come	**tiene miedo** = she or he is afraid
ir = to go	**el diagnosis** = the diagnosis
sacar = to take out	
hacer ejercicio = to exercise	
quedarse = to stay	

The Trunk (El Tronco)—Answers

1. **Tengo dolor del pecho hace una hora,** or
   Me duele el pecho hace una hora.
   I have had a pain in my chest for an hour.
2. **Hace dos meses que sufre de dolor de cabeza.**
   It makes two months that she suffers from headaches.
3. **El enfermero tiene que bañar al paciente.**
   The male nurse has to bathe the patient.
4. **El especialista va a examinar al paciente.**
   The specialist is going to examine the patient.
5. **La médica/doctora va a recetar/dar píldoras.**
   The female doctor is going to prescribe/give pills.
6. **El técnico va a sacar un rayo-X del pecho.**
   The male technician is going to take an X-ray of my chest.
7. **No me gusta hacer ejercicio.**
   I don't like to exercise.
8. **Tiene miedo del hospital.**
   He is afraid of the hospital.
9. **La enfermera quiere aprender español.**
   The female nurse wants to learn Spanish.
10. **Quiero hablar con la recepcionista.**
    I wish to speak with the receptionist.
11. **El paciente tiene que ir a la clínica hoy.**
    The male patient has to go to the clinic today.
12. **Tiene dolor y está muy nervioso.**
    He is in pain, and he is very nervous.
13. **Tienen que sacar/hacer más exámenes.**
    She has to take more tests.
14. **Mi madre tiene que quedarse en el hospital por una semana.**
    My mother has to stay in the hospital for a week.
15. **El médico va a hacer un diagnosis.**
    The male doctor is going to make a diagnosis.

The Organs (Los Órganos)—Written Practice

Now that you are able to translate directly from English to Spanish, generate the Spanish communication indicated by the English directions.

Example: Ask him if his head hurts.
¿Le duele la cabeza? ¿Tiene dolor de cabeza?

Situation 1: The patient has had an earache for three days.

1. Ask if it is a constant pain.
2. Tell him that you are going to examine his ears.
3. Tell him that he has to rest.
4. Tell him that he has to take some drops and some medicine that you are going to prescribe for him.
5. Ask him if he feels pain anywhere else.
6. Tell him that he must return in a week.

Situation 2: The patient has strong stomach pains.

1. Find out how long she has been in pain.
2. Ask her what she has been taking for the pain.
3. Ask her if she is constipated or if she (generally) suffers from constipation.
4. Ask her if she generally suffers from stomach pain.
5. Ask her if she eats well and has a good appetite.
6. Tell her that you need to take some tests.
7. Tell her that she must take the pills that you are going to prescribe.

Questions and Answers

1. What do you recommend for the pain?
2. He is taking the medicine now.
3. He suffers from lung disease.
4. They are going to take out his tonsils tomorrow.
5. She has an ear infection.
6. The doctor is going to examine her ears.

Word Bank

sufre = suffer

recomienda = recommend

necesito/es necesario = I need

The Organs (Los Órganos)—Answers

Situation 1: The patient has had an earache for three days.

1. **¿Tiene un dolor constante?**
   Ask if it is a constant pain.

2. **Voy a examinarle los oídos.**
   Tell him that you are going to examine his ears.

3. **Tiene que/Hay que descansar.**
   Tell him that he has to rest.

4. **Tiene que tomar gotas** (drops) **y medicina que voy a recetarle.**
   Tell him that he has to take some drops and medicine that you are going to prescribe for him.

5. **¿Se siente/Tiene dolor por otra parte?**
   Ask him if he feels pain anywhere else.

6. **Tiene que/hay que regresar en una semana.**
   Tell him that he must return in a week.

Situation 2: The patient has strong stomach pains.

1. **¿Cuánto tiempo hace que tiene dolor?**
   Find out how long she has been in pain.

2. **¿Toma medicina para el dolor?**
   Ask her what she has been taking for the pain.

3. **¿Está estriñido?**
   Ask her if she is constipated or if she (generally) suffers from constipation.
   ¿Puede hacer popo?

4. **¿Sufre dolor del estómago?**
   Ask her if she generally suffers from stomach pain.

5. **¿Come bien y tiene buen apetito?**
   Ask her if she eats well and has a good appetite.

6. **Es necesario tomar pruebas/exámenes.**
   Tell her that you need to take some tests.

7. **Hay que tomar píldoras que voy a recetarle.**
   Tell her that she must take the pills that you are going to prescribe.

Questions and Responses

1. **¿Qué recomienda para el dolor?**
   What do you recommend for the pain?
2. **Toma medicina ya.**
   He is taking the medicine now.
3. **Tiene enfermedad de los pulmones.**
   He suffers from lung disease.
4. **Van a sacar las amígdalas mañana.**
   They are going to take out his tonsils tomorrow.
5. **Tiene infección del oído.**
   She has an ear infection.
6. **El médico va a examinarle los oídos.**
   The doctor is going to examine her ears.

Reproduction

El Examen: La Contracepción—Written Practice

Speaker	Spoken Words
Paciente	I need a method of birth control. (**ante** = against, **conceptivo** = contraceptive)
Enfermero/ Enfermera	I am going to explain to you the various methods. The diaphragm is easy to use and is relatively effective in order to control birth (for birth control). The most effective is the pill.
Paciente	I would like to use the method of rhythm.
Enfermero/ Enfermera	It is necessary to understand how to use it correctly.
Paciente	Is it possible to explain to me?
Enfermero/ Enfermera	One needs to not have sexual relations some days before and after the fertile period.
Paciente	Is the method bad?
Enfermero/ Enfermera	One needs/must use additional protection—a condom.

Word Bank

más = more	**el más/la más** = the most
eficaz = effective	**más eficaz** = more effective
el más eficaz = the most effective	**relativamente** = relatively
controlar = to control	**natalidad** = birthrate
antes = before	**después** = after
método = method	**malo/bueno**= bad/good
examen = examination of patient	

Contraception Examination—Written Answers

Speaker	Spoken Words
Paciente	**Voy a necesitar un método anticonceptivo.** I need a method of birth control.
Enfermero/ Enfermera	**Voy explicarle los varios métodos.** I am going to explain to you the various methods.
	El diafragma es fácil de usar. The diaphragm is easy to use.
	El más eficaz es la píldora. The most effective is the pill.
	Es relativamente eficaz para controlar la natalidad. (It) is relatively effective to control birthrate.
Paciente	**Me gustaría usar un método de ritmo.** I would like to use the method of rhythm.
Enfermero/ Enfermera	**Es necesario entender usarlo correctamente.** It is necessary to understand how to use it correctly.
Paciente	**¿Es possible explicarme?** Is it possible to explain to me?
Enfermero/ Enfermera	**Hay que no tener relaciones unos días.** One needs to not have sexual relations some days.
	… antes y después del período fertile. … before and after the fertile period.
Paciente	**¿Es un método malo?** Is the method bad?
Enfermero/ Enfermera	**Hay que usar protection adicional—un condon.** One must use additional protection—a condom.

Past Pregnancies—Written Practice

Translate the following conversation into written Spanish. Remember that key words convey the message without needing to state the past tense. For example, "¿Otros embarazos?" ("Other pregnancies?")

Speaker	**Spoken Words**
Doctor	Have you had other pregnancies?
Patient	Yes.
Doctor	Have you had abortions?
Patient	No.
Doctor	Have you had other births?
Patient	Yes, twins.
Doctor	Have you used/taken contraceptives?
Patient	The pill, but not now.
Doctor	When did you quit taking the pill?
Patient	[It makes] six months ["ago" is understood].
Doctor	Do you have problems with pregnancy?
Patient	The baby has birth defects.
Doctor	Do you know why?
Patient	I have rubella during pregnancy.
Patient	It was a premature birth.
	My baby girl has to stay in the hospital.
Doctor	The weight?
Patient	Five pounds.

Past Pregnancies—Answers

Speaker	Spoken Words
Doctor	**¿Ha tenido otros embarazos?** Have you had other pregnancies?
Patient	**Sí.** Yes.
Doctor	**¿Ha tenido abortos?** Have you had abortions?
Patient	**No.** No.
Doctor	**¿Ha tenido otros partos?** Have you had other births?
Patient	**Sí, gemelos.** Yes, twins.
Doctor	**¿Ha usado/tomado contraceptivos?** Have you used/taken contraceptives?
Patient	**La píldora, pero ya no.** The pill, but not now.
Doctor	**¿Cuándo dejó de usar/tomar la píldora?** When did you quit taking the pill?
Patient	**Hace seis meses.** It makes six months [“ago” is understood].
Doctor	**¿Problemas con un embarazo?** Do you have problems with pregnancy?
Patient	**Si. Un bebé tiene defectos de nacimiento.** The baby has birth defects.
Doctor	**¿Sabe por qué?** Do you know why?
Patient	**Tengo rubella durante el embarazo** I have rubella during pregnancy.
Patient	**Fue un parto prematuro.** It was a premature birth.

	Mi nena tiene que quedarse en el hospitál. My baby girl has to stay in the hospital.
Doctor	**¿El peso?** The weight?
Patient	**Cinco libras.** Five pounds.

Word Bank: Below are expressions that you may find useful.

las almorranas/hemorroides = hemorrhoids/piles	**inyección intravenosa** = intravenous injection
la náusea = nausea	**el mareo** = dizziness
la anesthesia local = local anesthesia	**homorragia** = hemorrhage
el fórceps = forceps	**el flujo de sangre** = discharge of blood
criatura = infant	**las contracciones** = contractions
la partera = midwife	**calambres** = cramps
¿Sabe? = Does he/she know? Do you know?	**Sabe** = He/she knows, you know
el primer = the first (boy)	**la primera** = the first (girl)
el segundo = the second (boy)	**la segunda** = the second (girl)
el tercer = the third (boy)	**la tercera** = the third (girl)

Current Pregnancy—Written Practice

Translate the following dialogue between a patient and her nurse.

Speaker	**Spoken Words**
Patient	I am pregnant.
Doctor	How do you know?
Patient	I have not had a period for two months.
	And I have morning sickness.
Doctor	Do you have an appointment with the doctor?

Current Pregnancy—Answers

Speaker	**Spoken Words**
Paciente	**Estoy embarazada.** I am pregnant.
Enfermera	**¿Cómo sabe?** How do you know?
Paciente	**No tengo periodo por dos meses.** I don't have a period for two months.
	Y tengo nauseas. And I have nausea (morning sickness).
Enfermera	**¿Tiene una cita con el médico/médica?** Do you have an appointment with the doctor?

Labor and Delivery

Intake for Labor and Delivery—Written Practice

Speaker	Spoken Words
Médico/a	How do you feel?
Paciente	I'm in a lot of pain. My back hurts, and I have cramps.
Médico/a	Would you like to take something for the pain?
Paciente	¿Qué?
Médico/a	A sedative, an injection, or anesthesia.
	You have to relax yourself with breathing exercises.

Intake for Labor and Delivery—Answers

Speaker	Spoken Words
Médico/a	**¿Cómo se siente?** How do you feel?
Paciente	**Tengo mucho dolor.** I have much pain.
	Me duele la espalda y tengo calambres. My back hurts, and I have cramps.
Médico/a	**¿Le gustaría algo para el dolor?** Would you like something for the pain?
Paciente	**¿Qué?** What?
Médico/a	**Un sedante, una inyección, o una anestésia** A sedative, an injection, or anesthesia.
	Tiene que relajarse con ejercicios para respirar. You have to relax (yourself) with exercises for breathing.

Important:
You can use the transcript of Track 11, "Relaxation," to relax the patient.

Labor and Delivery—Written Practice

Note: Here, we dispense with the "Favor de" (the courteous sentence beginning) and instead give direct instructions.

The mother is ready to give birth. You give her the following information and directions.

Speaker	Spoken Words
Enfermera	We are going to the delivery room.
	When you have a contraction, inhale, hold your breath, and push.
	Ready? Let's count—one, two, three.
	Push and blow out!
	Relax!

Labor and Delivery—Answers

Speaker	Spoken Words
Enfermera	**Vamos a la sala de partos.** We are going to the delivery room.
	Cuando tenga una contracción, inhale, aguante la respiración, y empuje. When you have a contraction, inhale, hold the breath, and push.
	¿Lista? Vamos a contar—uno, dos, tres. Ready? Let's count—one, two, three.
	¡Empuje y sople! Push and blow out!
	¡Relajese! Relax!

Chapter 9: Using Spanish Numbers

Following, you will find two number charts. In Spanish, numbers above fifteen are expressed with "y," meaning "and." Thus, sixteen is expressed as ten and six, or *diez y seis*; twenty-one is expressed *veinte y uno*. Because of the linking of sounds, some numbers may be spelled as one word. Therefore, *diez y seis* is often spelled *dieciséis*, and twenty-one is spelled *veintiuno*, and so on. For clarity, I prefer the addition method of expressing numbers.

uno	one		*once*	eleven
dos	two		*doce*	twelve
tres	three		*trece*	thirteen
cuatro	four		*catorce*	fourteen
cinco	five		*quince*	fifteen
seis	six		*diez y seis*	sixteen
siete	seven		*diez y siete*	seventeen
ocho	eight		*diez y ocho*	eighteen
nueve	nine		*diez y nueve*	nineteen
diez	ten		*veinte*	twenty

When expressing numbers in the tens, one uses "y," meaning "and." However, in the hundreds place, one does not add "y." Thus, one hundred one is expressed *ciento uno*.

thirty	*treinta*		thirty-three	*treinta y tres*
forty	*cuarenta*		forty-four	*cuarenta y cuatro*
fifty	*cincuenta*		fifty-five	*cincuenta y cinco*
sixty	*sesenta*		sixty-six	*sesenta y seis*
seventy	*setenta*		seventy-seven	*setenta y siete*
eighty	*ochenta*		eighty-eight	*ochenta y ocho*
ninety	*noventa*		ninety-nine	*noventa y nueve*
hundred	*cien*		one hundred one	*ciento uno*

Excellent Website for Studying Numbers

If you are not able to count in Spanish, use this site to learn how: http://www.studyspanish.com/lessons/cardnum3.htm

Use Numbers in Medical Communications

You use numbers in many medical communications, as shown in the following tables.

Speak the words in the Spanish column three times, slowly.

Category	Number	Spanish	English
Age	21	**Tengo veintiún años.***	I am twenty-one.
Pain level (1 to 10)	7	**Siete**	Seven
Weight	125	**Ciento veinticinco libras**	125 pounds
Height	5'	**Cinco pies**	Five feet
	5'4"	**Cinco pies, cuatro pulgadas**	Five feet, four inches
Pulse	67	**Sesenta y siete**	Sixty-seven
Temperature	99º	**Noventa y nueve grados**	Ninety-nine degrees
Blood pressure	120/80	**Ciento veinte sobre ochenta**	One hundred twenty over eighty

*You may also hear "Tengo veintiuno."

Category	Numeral	Spanish	English
Time	1:00	**Es la una.**	It is one o'clock.
	2:00	**Son las dos.**	It is two o'clock.
	3:00	**Son las tres.**	It is three o'clock.
Price	$5.00	**¿Cuánto cuesta?** **Cinco dólares.**	How much does it cost? Five dollars.

Communicate about Time

Excellent Website for Learning How to Tell Time

If you are not able to tell time in Spanish, use the following site to learn how: http://www.studyspanish.com/lessons/time.htm

What Time Is It?—¿Qué Hora Es?

To ask the current time, you say:
¿Qué hora es?

To state the current time, you say:
"**Es la una**" or "**Son las dos/tres/cuatro/cinco … doce.**"

1. Ask the question below and answer with each answer in the table.
2. Ask the question again and answer with times not listed below.

Question	Answer
¿Qué hora es? What hour (time) is it?	**Es la una.** It is one o'clock. **Son las dos menos quince/quarto.** There are two [hours] minus fifteen [minutes]. (In English, we say, "It is a quarter of two.") **Son las dos menos veinte.** There are two [hours] minus twenty [minutes]. **Son las cuatro de la tarde.** It is four in the afternoon. **Son las siete de la noche.** It is seven in the evening. **Son las once y media de la noche.** It is eleven thirty in the evening. **Son las dos y cinco de la mañana.** It is two-oh-five in the morning.

On the radio you will hear people say:

- **Faltan veinte para las dos.**
  Lacking twenty minutes until two.
- **Falta un cuarto para las tres.**
  Lacking fifteen minutes until three.

When Is an Event?—¿Cuándo Es? ¿A Qué Hora?
To state the time for an appointment, you say:

La cita (the appointment) **es a** (is at)

- **la una/las dos/las tres**, etc. (hour)
- **de la mañana/tarde** (of the morning/afternoon)
- **el cinco/seis**, etc. (day of the month)
- **de mayo/junio**, etc. (of month)

Example: La cita es a las tres y media de la tarde el dos de mayo.

1. Ask each question below and answer with an answer in the table.
2. Ask each question again and answer with times not listed below.

Beginning	Event	Answer
¿Cuándo es … When is … **¿A qué hora es …** At what hour is …	**la cita?** the appointment? **el rayo-X?** the X-ray? **el examen?** the examination? **la cirugía?** the surgery?	**A la una.** At one o'clock. **A la una y diez.** At one ten. **A la una y cuarto.** At a quarter after one. **A la una y quince.** At one fifteen. **A la una y veinticinco.** At one twenty-five. **A la una y media.** At one and a half. **A la una y treinta.** At one thirty. **A las dos menos veinte.** At two o'clock minus twenty minutes (or twenty to two). **A veinte para las dos.** At twenty minutes until two.

Before and After—Antes de y Después de

To identify a time before or after an *event*, you say:

"**Antes de** la cita" or "**Después de** el rayo-X"

Combine words: **Beginning + Action + Before/After + Event**.

Beginning	Action	Before/After	Event
Favor de Please **Es necesario** It is necessary	**llegar** to arrive **pagar** to pay **esperar** to wait **poner el camisón** to put on the gown	**antes de** before **después de** after	**la cita.** the appointment. **el rayo-X.** the X-ray. **el examen.** the examination. **la cirugia.** the surgery.

To identify a time before or after a *time*, you say:

"**Antes de** la una" or "**Después de** tres semanas."

Combine words: **Beginning + Action + Before/After + Time**.

Beginning	Action	Before/After	Time
Favor de Please	**llegar** arrive	**antes de** before	**las seite y media.** seven thirty.
Es necesario It is necessary	**pagar** pay	**después de** after	**diez días.** ten days.
	esperar hasta wait		**seis semanas.** six weeks.
			cuatro meses. four months.
			dos años. two years.

Chapter 10: Using "Hace"

How Long?—Hace + Action Word in Present

To ask how long since the patient has had a symptom, you say:

¿Cuánto tiempo + hace que + tiene + [the symptom]?
How much time + does it make that + you have + [the symptom]?

Example:

¿Cuánto tiempo hace que tiene calentura?
How much time does it make that you have a fever?

To answer, the patient says:

Hace + [a time expression].

Example: **Hace tres días.**

1. Ask the question for each symptom listed. As you ask the questions, touch the words and stand up.
2. Give two answers to each question. As you answer, touch the words and sit down.

Begin Question	... Symptom?	Answer
¿Cuánto tiempo hace que tiene ... How much time does it make that you have... (How long have you had ...)	**dolor de cabeza?** pain of head? **dolor de estómago?** pain of stomach? **mal estar?** bad feeling/feel bad? **calambres?** cramps? **calentura?** fever? **escalofríos?** chills?	**Una hora.** One hour. **Dos horas y media.** Two and a half hours. **Medio día.** Half a day. **Nueve horas.** Nine hours. **Todo la noche.** All night. **Cuatro días.** Four days.

Or you can ask **¿Cuánto tiempo hace?** (How long does it make?)
Some patients answer,

Hace + [time expresión] + que tengo + [symptom].

It makes + [time expression] + I have + the symptom.

Example:

Hace	**una semana**	**que**	**tengo dolor de estómago.**
(It makes	a week	that	I have stomachache.)

Ask, **¿Cuánto tiempo hace?**
Answer by combining words from the columns:

Hace + [time expression] + que tengo + [symptom].
Speak an answer using each time and symptom listed.

Hace + [time expression] + que tiene + [symptom].
Speak an answer using each time and symptom listed.

Hace	Time	Que	Symptom
Hace ... It makes (It has been ...)	**una hora** one hour **dos horas y media** two and a half hours **medio día** half a day **nueve horas** nine hours **toda la noche** all the night **cuatro días** four days	**que tengo** since I have **que tiene** since he/she has	**dolor de cabeza.** pain of head. **dolor de estómago.** pain of stomach/ stomachache. **mal estar.** bad feeling/feel bad. **calambres.** cramps. **calentura.** fever. **escalofríos.** chills. **picazón.** itching. **pies hinchados.** swollen feet.

How Long Ago?—Hace + Action Word in Past

Hace also refers to **how long ago** something happened.

To ask how much time has passed since something happened, say:

¿Cuánto tiempo hace + que + [past action]?

Examples:

- **¿Cuánto tiempo** **hace que** **se enfermó?**
  How much time does it make that you became ill?

- **¿Cuánto tiempo** **hace que** **vomitó?**
  How much time does it make that you vomited?

To answer, you say:

Hace + [a time expression] + que + [past action].

Question		Answer	
Begin Question	**Past Action**	**Hace**	**Time**
¿Cuánto tiempo hace que … How much time does it make that… (How long ago …)	**comió?** he/she/you ate? **tomó?** he/she/you drank? **vomitó?** he/she/you vomited? **durmió?** he/she/you slept? **se quemó?** he/she/you burned?	**Hace …** It has been …	**una hora.** one hour. **dos horas y media.** two and a half hours. **medio día.** half a day. **nueve horas.** nine hours. **toda la noche.** all the night. **cuatro días.** four days.

Conclusion

I studied Spanish for years without being able to speak it. It was similar to a math course. I could rattle off the conjugations as I had with math tables. But I worried about using perfect grammar and never made a beginning.

Using this book you will begin to communicate in Spanish with patterns unique to the language, substituting new words to make new expressions. As you master pronunciation, you will be able to give the intake exam and clinical history. Through listening to the CD, you will acquire additional vocabulary. You will now be able to create language through the mix-and-match tables and communicate without cumbersome conjugation. Also, you will be able to practice using the written exercises and verify your answers. You can combine phrases from the procedural explanations and create new communication, as with the mix-and-match tables.

May you find satisfaction in making effective contributions to the health care delivery system through communicating in the language of your patients.

About the Author

Murnez Blades is a bilingual and bicultural educator, fluent in reading, writing, and speaking Spanish and English. She earned her BA from Baylor University and later completed an MA from the University of San Francisco.

Inspired by her grandfather, Grande, who rode on cattle trains into Mexico, Murnez studied in Mexico City in her early twenties. And so began her passion for Hispanic culture and language. Spanish language and culture is her vocation and her avocation. Paul Molina, her son-in-law, once commented, "You are more Hispanic than I am!"

While serving as a translator with medical outreach programs to Mexico, she recognized the need for medical Spanish communication. She now teaches her Spanish communication program at Goldenwest College in Huntington Beach, California.

Her studies in Mexico have included live-in programs in Cuernavaca and Oaxaca, Mexico, and in San Jose, Costa Rica. Her passion for the culture led Murnez to know Fidelia, a *curandera* (healer), who shared some of her secrets and taught Murnez to respect this healing art in addition to, or as a complement to, traditional medical treatment.

While teaching, Murnez developed a cost-effective cross-cultural program with both day excursions to and a live-in study in Baja, California, and travels to Spain.

With over forty years of teaching experience, Ms. Blades remains passionate about creating motivational instruction for her students. In her company, Camino Español, she teaches "Spanish for Fun and Forever" to adults, youths, and even three-year-olds.

To purchase the CD and/or book, please go to www.caminoespanol.com, or write to Ms. Murnez Blades at 18422 Carnaby Lane, Huntington Beach, CA 92648.

Notes

---

[1] Susan M. Heathfield, "Listen with Your Eyes: Tips for Understanding Nonverbal Communication," About.com Human Resources, http://humanresources.about.com/od/interpersonalcommunicatio1/a/nonverbal_com.htm.

[2] Stella Vosniadou, "How Children Learn," Educational Practice Series 7 (International Bureau of Education, 2001), http://www.ibc.unesco.org/fileadmin/user_upload/archive/publications/EducationalPracticesSeriesPdf/prac07e.pdf.

[3] Elizabeth B. Bernhardt, "Teaching Other Languages," Educational Practice Series 20 (International Bureau of Education, 2010), http://www.ibe.unesco.org/fileadmin/user_upload/Publications/Educational_Practices/EdPractices_20.pdf.

[4] National Training Laboratories (NTL) Institute for Applied Behavioral Science, Learning Pyramid, http://homepages.gold.ac.uk/polovina/learnpyramid/about.htm.

[5] Eric Jensen, *Brain-Based Learning* (Thousand Oaks, CA: Corwin Press, 2008), 105–12.

[6] Rachel Mattison, "Different Kinds of Music That Affect Your Memory While Studying," last updated April 20, 2012, http://www.ehow.com/list_5965674_different-music-affect-memory-studying.html.

[7] James Asher, *Listen and Perform in Spanish: The TPR Student Book* (Los Gatos, CA: Sky Oaks Productions, 1991).

[8] Ben Shearon, "James Asher's Total Physical Reponse: A Short Introduction," http://www.c-english.com/files/tpr.pdf.

[9] Elena Avila, *Woman Who Glows in the Dark: A Curandera Reveals Traditional Aztec Secrets of Physical and Spiritual Health* (New York: Penguin, 1999).
For a short video, see http://www.youtube.com/watch?v=kZl_qzbGVRI.

[10] Maria Antonia Di Lorenzo-Kearon and Thomas P. Kearon, *Medical Spanish: A Conversational Approach* (Orlando, FL: Holt, Rinehart and Winston, 1981), 109.